Fundamentals of Economics: Making Your Way in Our Economy

Daniel Francis Hess

Student Edition

The Center for Learning

Author

Daniel Francis Hess teaches economics, world history, and American history at the secondary level. He earned his M.S. from Cleveland State University. This is his first Center for Learning curriculum unit.

The Publishing Team

Rose Schaffer, M.A., President/Chief Executive Officer
Bernadette Vetter, M.A., Vice President
Lora Murphy, M.A., Vice President, Social Studies Division
Tammy Sanderell, B.A., Editor

Cover Design

Susan Chowanetz Thornton, B.S.

Dedication

This book is dedicated to Bob, Maureen, Julia, and Bill Ryan and their faith in me.

List of credits found on Acknowledgments page beginning on 247.

ISBN 1-56077-659-5

Contents

		Page	Handout
Part 1: Basics in Economics			
1	Basics in Economics	7	1
	How Big?	23	2
2	The Factors of Production	26	3
3	Our Economy in Operation	29	4
4	Graphing Supply and Demand	32	5
5	Graphing Problems	34	6
6	Thought Questions	41	7
Part 2: Business and Labor			
7	Business and Labor	48	8
	Business Basics	64	9
8	Business Organizations	69	10
9	Beginning in Business	72	11
10	Business Flow Chart	74	12
11	Monopolies	77	13
12	The Sherman Antitrust Act	80	14
13	Labor Research Assignment	85	15
14	Supply and Demand for Labor	89	16
Part 3: Financial Institutions			
15	Financial Institutions	96	17
	Reading and Vocabulary	114	18
16	Mind on Your Money	119	19
17	You and the CPI	123	20
18	Basic Monetary Policy	127	21
19	Monetary Policy in Action	131	22
20	The Chairman of the Fed Speaks	134	23
Part 4: Government and the Economy			
21	Government and the Economy	141	24
	Reading and Vocabulary	155	25
22	Doing Your Taxes	159	26
23	Problems and Solutions	162	27
24	The Layers of Government	164	28

25	Political Cartoons	166	29
26	My Government Research	169	30
27	Take a Stand?	173	31
Part 5: Personal Finance			
28	Personal Finance	179	32
	The Language of Personal Finance	199	33
29	My Checkbook	202	34
30	My Budget	204	35
31	You and Your Loans	206	36
32	The Language of Wall Street	210	37
33	Investing	212	38
34	Reading a Business Page	214	39
35	The Challenge	216	40
Part 6: Global and Ethical Perspectives			
36	Global and Ethical Perspectives	221	41
	Reading and Vocabulary	233	42
37	Global Perspectives	236	43
38	Economist's Views	238	44
39	Ethical Dilemmas	241	45
40	My Beliefs	244	46
Bibliography		245	

Part 1
Basics in Economics

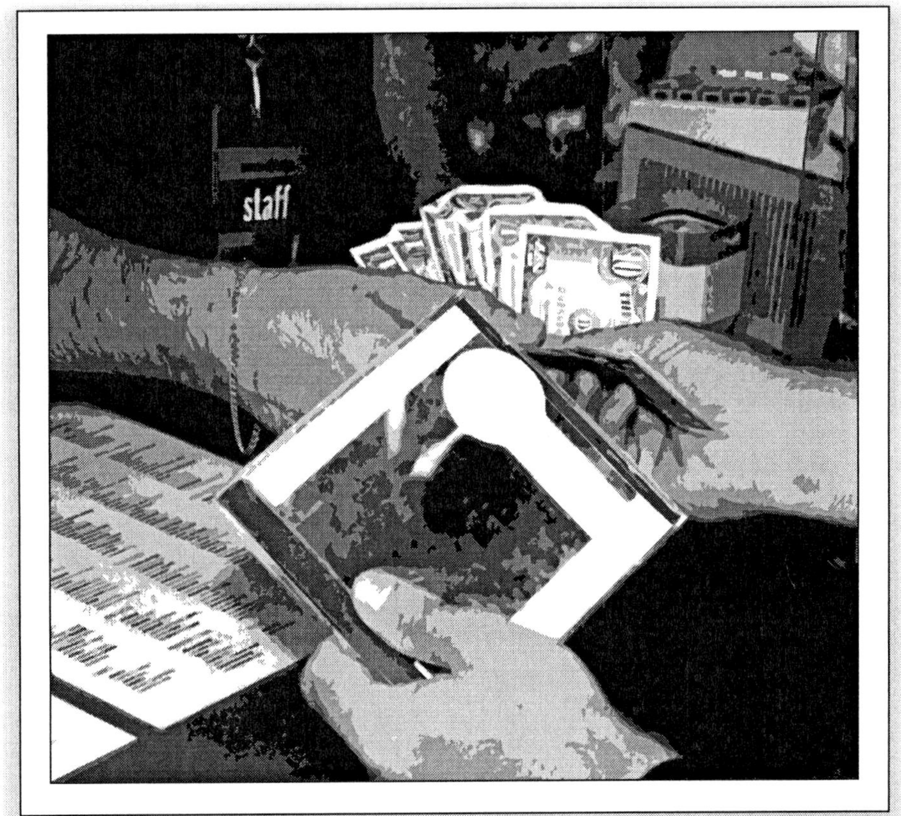

Questions to Consider

1. What is an economy?
2. Who gets what and why? Why is there poverty?
3. What is the difference between a good and bad economy?
4. What are the differences between supply and demand?
5. Can an economy be measured and predicted?
6. How can an economy grow?
7. How are our lives affected by the economy?
8. What happens when we try to influence the economy?
9. Why are some countries so poor?

Terms You Need in Order to Read

Economy
Supply
Demand
Economics
Elasticity
Scarcity
Recession

Name____________________________

Date____________________________

Basics in Economics

Directions: Read the selection, and answer the Pressing Questions as you read. Be prepared for class discussion.

A. What Is the Economy?

How many times have you heard people discussing the economy? The conversations were probably enough to bore you to tears. For many reasons, people everywhere discuss and watch the economy quite closely. They might say that the economy is "bad," or that economic conditions are getting worse. Conversely, you may hear that the economy is doing very well and growing. To understand what that means exactly, you need to know a few simple concepts.

Think about the Great Depression. It is easy to say that our economy has never been worse since the turn of the twentieth century. One of the main symptoms of our floundering economic state was a high rate of unemployment. There were few jobs available for our labor force. If few people are working, then that must mean that very little is being produced. In other words, there is little production of goods and services. There was a depressed level of buying and a low level of production. For many reasons, this condition lasted for more than ten years.

Simply put, an **economy** is a situation in which people produce goods and then other people consume those **goods**. In our modern economy, it is important to realize that material goods are not the only things that people can consume. **Services** are actions or activities that are done for others. While Ford and GM make cars for consumption by their customers, lawyers and accountants provide services that their customers need. No matter what one does for a living, we are all subject to the swings in the economy.

The Pressing Questions

1. When the economy is in a slump, what do you think are some of the impacts on our society?

2. Write a definition for *bad economy.*

When an economy produces and consumes at a high rate, it allows some people to spend extra cash on luxuries.

B. Scarcity and Opportunity Cost

The fundamental problem of economics is **scarcity**. In our world, people have unlimited desires and wants, but our resources are too limited to satisfy them. The resulting condition leaves people with a multitude of difficult decisions. We all have **wants and needs**. Our needs include things like food and shelter. They are necessary to our survival. Cars and fancy clothes may be wants that people have. They are not vital to life, but we desire them just the same. Every day, we must make decisions, based upon our resources, about how to satisfy our wants and needs.

Competition exists because of the scarcity of goods. There is an inherent limited supply of resources that we desire. People may want many goods and services, but there are never enough to go around. For instance, if you decide to buy a new Walkman, that may mean you will not have enough money for prom. You have a limited amount of money available. If you spend it on one thing, it will not be available for another. This dilemma is fundamental to the study of economics.

The difficult choice between alternatives for our available resources will sometimes result in sacrifice. For example, suppose you have the opportunity to go to a baseball game and you want to go. However, a new group that you really enjoy is giving a concert at the same time the game is scheduled. You realize that you have time and money to do only one of the two. You have a difficult choice to make. In the end, you have to weigh all the options. Your team may be in the playoffs, but you've never seen this band before. The opportunity cost of attending the concert is not being able to attend the game. The opportunity cost of attending the game is not being able to attend the concert. You must choose on over the other. Such is life, and such is economics.

In the end, you have to figure out which one is more important. You will have to sacrifice one of the two. The losses and benefits of your decision are called **trade-offs**. Let's say you decided to go to the concert. It was a lot of fun, and you even made some new friends. However, you notice in the paper the next day that your team won in the last minutes of the game. This may have been a rather tough sacrifice. The cost of what you sacrifice is called the **opportunity cost**. In this case, the price was rather high.

The previous example is rather simple. There are only two things to choose from. Imagine if you are in charge of a large corporation and you need to build some new factories. There will be numerous resources that must be allocated and many trade-offs will need to be considered. Sometimes, economists are consulted when large decisions like this are required. In actuality, they are not consulted enough.

The Pressing Question

3. a. If you decide to get a job right after high school that pays $22,000 per year instead of going to college, what are some of the trade-offs and opportunity costs in the immediate future?

   b. What about the trade-offs and opportunity costs over long-term?

Grand monuments like those in Egypt were built by societies that produced great wealth. Leaders diverted resources to their own projects.

C. Types of Economies

Whenever people live together, economies will develop. From the earliest river valley civilizations, we can easily see that certain people would spend most of their time growing crops while other people developed specialized skills. They were affected by scarcity just as nations today are forced to make decisions about trade-offs. It is the people of a nation who often determine how to best use a country's resources.

There are a variety of basic decisions that must be made when it comes to running a nation's economy. First of all, a country must decide on how much freedom to give its citizens to make decisions on their own. Second, citizens and their leaders have to decide what goods will be produced or services will be provided. Third, the difficult question of how the goods are to be distributed must be answered. An **economic system** is an organized set of procedures and practices that a society follows in the production and distribution of goods and services. In our world, economists have identified four types:

- A **traditional economy** relies on customs to answer these questions. Customs, religion, and laws aid in the passing of skills from parent to child. Change happens slowly because people are reluctant to move from how things were done in the past. Some of these systems still exist in Africa, Latin America, and the Middle East.
- **Command economies** rely on powerful government officials, often named *central planners,* to make economic decisions. They decide on how goods will be produced and how much of each will end up in the hands of the citizens. The individual citizen usually has to defer to the leaders on most economic matters. For example, in ancient Egypt, the pharaoh controlled all aspects of production and distribution. He owned all of the land and collected all of the taxes. In the European Middle Ages, lords of the manor exercised similar power.
- A **pure market economy** relies on the individual to make the economic decisions. The government has little say in what is produced, sold, or consumed. The system relies on "the market" to provide enough resources to keep things going. A market is where goods and services are exchanged freely. People are motivated by self-interest.
- Economies today are classified as **mixed economies.** This is because they combine aspects of the pure market and command systems. In a **capitalist** economy, as in the United States today, individuals own and control the resources, but the government does have some control of the economy through taxation and regulations. Nations that are closer to the command-style economy are known as **authoritarian socialist** or **communist.** The government controls all of the resources and makes all economic decisions. Cuba is communist today despite the fact that individuals are making more economic decisions for themselves.

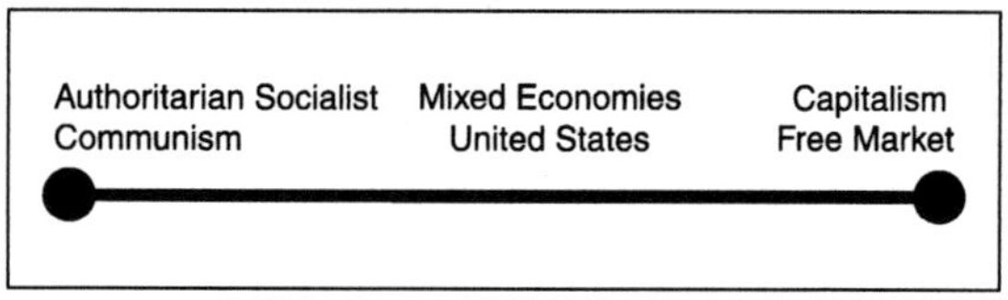

The Pressing Question

4. Evaluate the economic system of the United States. List and explain a few of its strengths and weaknesses.

D. Who Gets What and Why?

Something might have occurred to you as you read the last section. Each of the four systems addressed in the previous section answers the question, "who gets what and why?" While that is putting it rather simply, it captures the essence of what economics is all about. Economists are fascinated with how people deal with the fact that goods and services are inherently scarce.

The study of the allocation of those scarce resources is known as economics. For example, while the United States has less than five percent of the world's population, we consume over one-third of the world's food. How is that possible? Is there a lot of waste involved? How did we gain such prominence? How do we maintain such control? These are all questions that an economist would venture to ask. The answers are more elusive than you might think.

Also, why are there still poor people in the United States? Some people think that they are in that situation by choice, but most of the time, the answers are more complex than that. Regardless of your views, the fact remains that for one reason or another, some people have lots of stuff, and other people do not. This is what economics is all about. Economists struggle to figure out why goods and services are distributed unevenly. The questions are that much more difficult when you consider that our economy is constantly changing.

As our world has become increasingly complex, our professions and occupations have become increasingly specialized. The field of economics is no exception. In college, you will have the option of taking classes called **microeconomics** and **macroeconomics.** Micro, as it is called, concerns itself with the decisions made by individuals and businesses. Macro, on the other hand, is primarily concerned with economics on a national or global scale. If you wanted to learn about how our national government uses its resources, you would study macroeconomics. If you wanted to learn how to make a small business run more efficiently, you should study microeconomics. For most business majors today, both courses are required for graduation.

The Pressing Question

5. How can the United States control so much of the world's resources? Why do we have it so good?

E. The Factors of Production

Think about a car that you might want to buy at some time in the future. How did the company actually put it together? They needed steel and plastic. Workers labored on assembly lines to put it together. Computers and

ECONOMICS

Course and Program Information: 555-4520

A.	ECN	201	1	PRIN OF MACROECO	4	9:45A-10:50A	MWF	102	GARCIA	100
A.	ECN	201	2	PRIN OF MACROECO	4	10:00A-11:50A	T TH	211	STAFF	75
A.	ECN	201	3	PRIN OF MACROECO	4	11:00A-12:05P	MWF	409	SMITH	100
#A.	**ECN**	**201**	**50**	**PRIN OF MACROECO**	**4**	**6:00 P-7:50P**	**M W**	**105**	**STAFF**	**75**
B.	ECN	202	1	PRIN OF MICROECO	4	9:45A-10:50A	MWF	211	VEBLEN	100
B.	ECN	202	2	PRIN OF MICROECO	4	12:15P-1:20P	MWF	409	STAFF	100
#B.	**ECN**	**202**	**50**	**PRIN OF MICROECO**	**4**	**6:00P-7:50P**	**M W**	**102**	**STAFF**	**75**
C.	ECN	301	1	INTER MACROECON	4	12:15P-1:20P	T TH	409	SMITH	50
C.	ECN	302	1	PRICE THEORY 1	4	9:45A-10:50A	MWF	426	STAFF	50
#C.	**ECN**	**302**	**2**	**PRICE THEORY 1**	**4**	**6:00P-7:50P**	**M W**	**409**	**SMITH**	**60**
D.	ECN	355	1	MONEY & BANKING	4	10:00A-11:50A	MWF	102	GARCIA	100

Most colleges offer a variety of economics classes.

some advanced technology made the production process more efficient and cost-effective. The owners of the company risked their own time and money on the success of the venture. If any of these factors were missing, the car could not be produced. This is the reason they are called the **factors of production**.

Sometimes called the means of production, they are as follows:

- **Labor**—the application of human physical and mental talent to the production process
- **Natural resources**—items provided by mother nature
- **Capital**—the cash, tools, equipment, and machinery needed in the production process; technology, or the new methods and applications of the science of production, also fits in this category.
- **Entrepreneurs**—Finally, you need someone to put it all together. Someone has to take the risk. It is often the most important factor of production. A person's creativity, capital, know-how, and personal drive are instrumental to success.

Without all four of the factors of production, it is impossible to provide a good or service. Some economists, like Karl Marx, believed that those who can control these factors can exploit those who do not. In any case, knowing them is key to understanding economics. Each factor of production is scarce.

The Pressing Question

6. Look around the room you are in right now. Choose a consumer product, preferably one that you bought yourself. For each of the factors of production, give some details as to how that product came into being. (For an example, reread the first part of the section.)

Because of changing technology, less than three percent of the workforce in the United States works on farms. Food production is still vital to our economy.

F. Simple Concepts of Demand

When you first chose to take economics, you probably thought very little of the prospect. What may have come to mind are the three words "supply and demand." We need to look at these concepts very closely. And as you are going to realize, they are very different.

Because economics is a **social science**, it depends on accurate figures to determine what is occurring in the marketplace, and, even more importantly, to make predictions about the future. For that reason, economists do not consider demand simply wanting something. This is difficult to calculate. Rather, we define **demand** as the amount of a good or service that people are willing and able to buy at a given price and during a certain time period.

Businesses need accurate figures to plan what to do in the future. You may want to buy a Lexus when you get out of college, but that will probably not be an option. You desire the car, but you do not have the money or the credit. Feelings of consumers are fleeting and somewhat hard to gauge. Sales figures are hard data that help a company predict what will happen in the future.

The **law of demand** states that an increase in price will bring a decrease in quantity demanded, while a decrease in price will cause an increase in quantity demanded. It all comes down to common sense. If compact discs go from an average of $12 per unit to $24 per unit, the quantity demanded for CDs will inevitably go down, other things being equal. If there is a big sale on CDs, and they drop in price to $8 apiece, the quantity demanded would be much greater. Again, this would be evident through the sales figures. No matter what the situation, a change in price will bring a change in the quantity demanded.

Because there is an inverse relationship between price and quantity, a graph of the law of demand will yield a curve with a negative slope. Consider the information on the **demand schedule** below:

Demand for CD Players

Price	Quantity
$250	0
$230	1,000
$210	2,000
$190	3,000
$170	4,000
$150	5,000
$130	6,000

Notice the nature of the information. As the figures in the Price (P) column go up, the figures in the Quantity (Q) go down. In economics, it is possible to graph information and discover the nature of the demand of a certain product. Inspect the graph below:

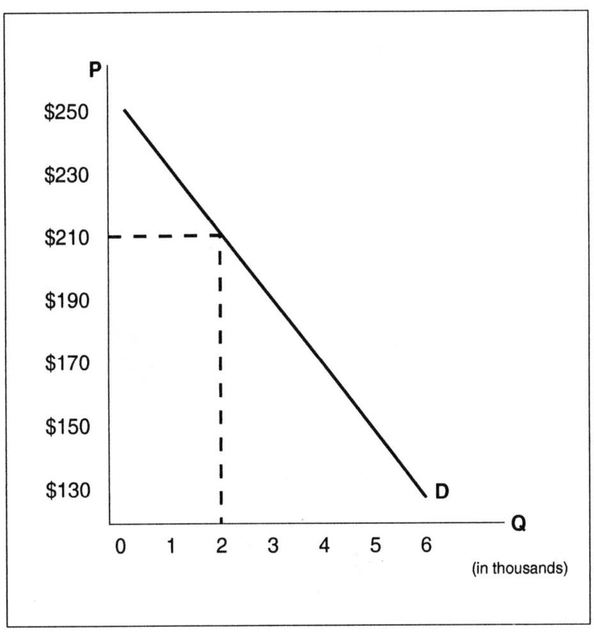

The Pressing Question

7. In usual circumstances, your school sells 3,000 tickets to its football games at $5 each. Fill out the chart below for what you believe the quantity demanded would be as the ticket prices rose or fell.

Price in dollars	Amount Sold
3	________
4	________
5	3,000
6	________

G. Changes in Price Affect Quantity Demanded

Think about a rubber band. The more elastic it is, the more it can stretch. If a product changes its price, we expect there will be a change in the quantity demanded. Economists call the degree of that change a product's **elasticity**. Look to the graph below. This is an example of an elastic demand curve.

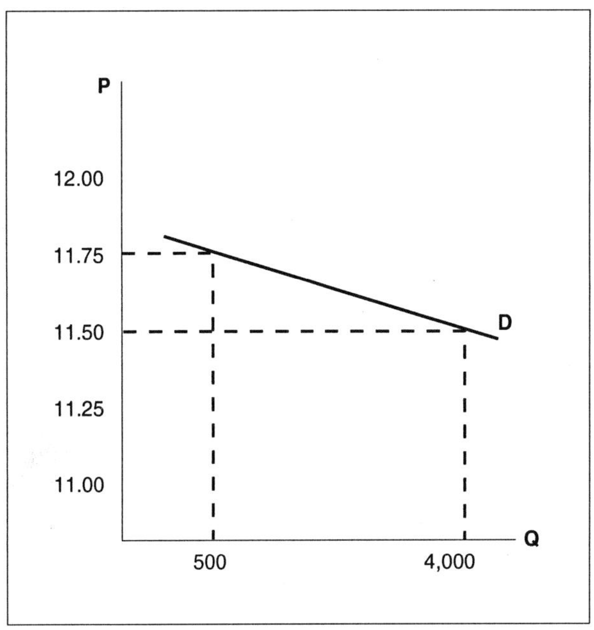

When the price changed only a little, the quantity demanded changed a whole lot. Economists would say that this product has an

elastic demand. This is because people will make the decision not to buy the product if it does not fit in their budgets.

On the other hand, there are products that are necessary to our survival. We call these **necessities**. For example, if you had a pacemaker, and had to replace the battery every so often, a slight jump in price would not dissuade you from buying one. In fact, a great jump in price might not bother you either. Paying a lot for a battery is better than a massive heart attack any day. No matter what happens to price, the quantity demanded will remain rather constant. Look at the following graph.

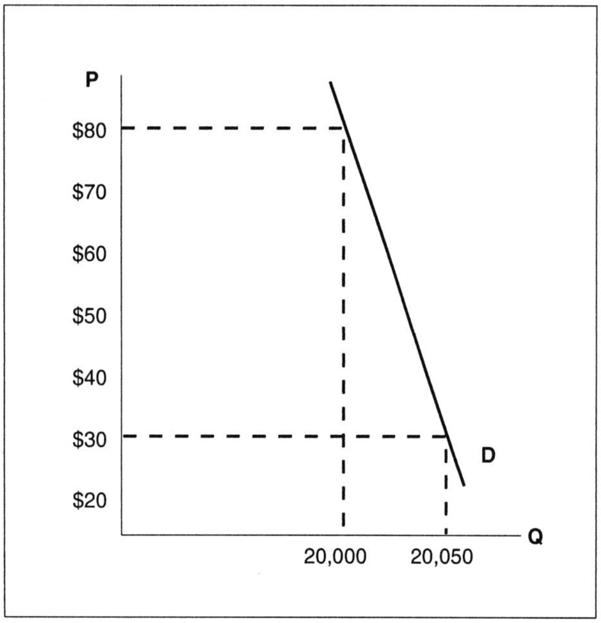

Notice that when the price increases or decreases on the y-axis, that the quantity on the x-axis hardly moves. Economists would say that pacemaker battery sales are quite price inelastic.

How inelastic the demand for a certain product is depends greatly upon how much people need or want the product. **Utility** is the usefulness or satisfaction that people get from a good or service. For example, coffee in the morning might have a very low utility for you while the thought of a donut gets you giddy to the point of hysteria. Donuts have more utility. One would expect that you would have a constant lust for donuts. This is not the case.

Imagine that feeling you get when you eat that first one. It's your favorite—glazed, with a jelly filling. The first one is magic going down, but as you eat the second one, you find that it is not as satisfying. Subsequently, each one that you gorge loses its appeal more and more. This is known as **diminishing marginal utility**. In other words, the utility you get from pastry to pastry will decrease with each one you eat.

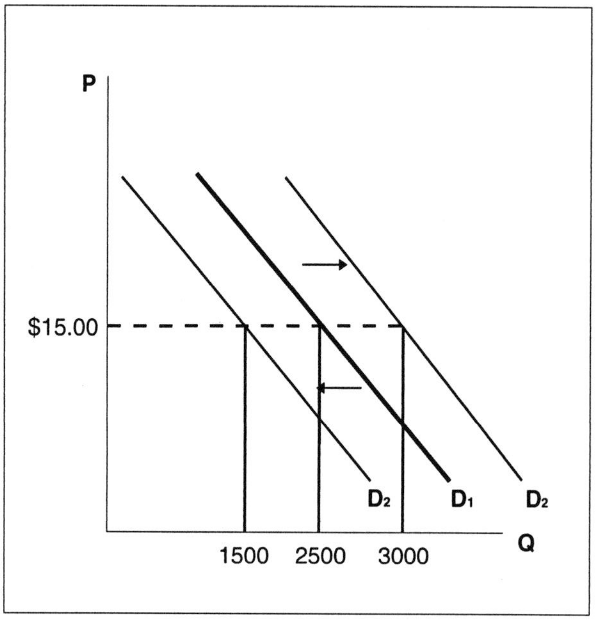

Lastly, when you venture out on your own into the "real world," what do you suppose you will eat? Many college students who live on a shoestring budget eat generic goods and inexpensive foods like macaroni and cheese. They dream of the day when their budgets no longer constrain their diets. Products that one buys less of when income rises are called **inferior**. This **income effect** on demand also has a flip side. As people make more money, there are some products they tend to buy more often. These are called **normal goods.** Most students don't have money for luxurious items like steak and shrimp, but once they graduate and begin collecting a paycheck, their budgets may permit it.

The Pressing Question

8. List five products that have elastic demands and five products that have inelastic demands.

H. Demand Curves Move!

Over a period of time, the simple demand curves that we've been studying may shift from left to right. In other words, it is possible for sales of CDs to increase while remaining at a set price of $12 apiece. Maybe the bands today are more popular. Perhaps the average music buyer has more money to spend. Perhaps consumers will begin to prefer another medium. We call these factors that change the quantity demanded without a change in price the **determinants of demand**. There are five of them that will be discussed:

- **Consumer preferences**—In 1987, New Kids on the Block sold tons of merchandise. But as tastes have changed in the last decade, they sell next to nothing outside of garage sales any more.
- **Market size**—As the baby boomers start to reach their golden years, the demand for Depends Undergarments will go up. The prices can remain the same, but with more senior citizens, the quantity demanded will increase.
- **Income**—If the average income of the average family goes down, then we can expect sales in the school bookstore to drop. Students will simply not have the money to spend on sweatshirts and diskettes.
- **Prices of related goods**—If the price of Skippy goes up, people will simply buy more Peter Pan or Jif. We call products easily replaced with others **substitutes.**

  On the other hand, if the price of all peanut butter goes up by five times, people will buy less. If that happens, Smuckers will no doubt experience a sharp decrease in sales. Peanut butter and jelly are often sold in conjunction with one another. We call them **complements**.
- **Consumer security**—Most adults have a certain amount of anxiety about the future. When people feel good about the future, they tend to spend money. When they feel that they might lose their jobs or that a depression might be coming soon, they will not buy as much. This would decrease the amount of sales a store would have while they never adjusted their price.

Study the following graph.

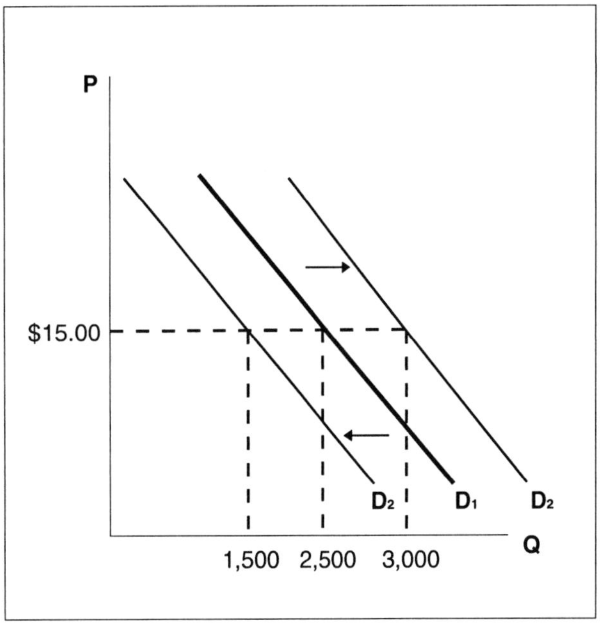

Try to determine which one has increasing demand and which one has the decreasing demand. Notice that the price remained constant at $15, but the quantity changed from the initial 2,500.

The Pressing Question

9. Considering school cafeteria cheeseburgers, for each of the five determinants, state one instance for each of the five determinants in which demand would increase or decrease.

I. Supply in the Marketplace

It is time to think like a producer or seller of products. People go into business to make a **profit.** After all of the expenses have been paid, one hopes to have a significant amount of money left over. When consumers want a product at a certain price, a good business will do everything in its power to fill that demand. If consumers are willing to spend more, there is good opportunity for higher profits. Businesses will increase production to meet the higher demand. Thus, the **law of supply** states that an *increase* in price will result in an increase in the quantity supplied while a *decrease* in price will cause a decrease in the amount supplied.

The supply relationship between price and quantity is positive. Therefore, see if you notice this relationship as you look at the **supply schedule** below:

Supply Schedule for CD Players

Price	Quantity
$90	0
$110	1,000
$130	2,000
$150	3,000
$170	4,000
$190	5,000
$210	6,000

Did you notice that as the P figures increased, so did the Q figures? An increase in price may dictate an increase in profits if costs stay the same. It is important to think like a producer of products when considering supply. The object of business is to make a profit. So, if the market is offering a higher price for your product, you would increase production. This could mean higher profits for you. If you choose not to increase production, with the higher price on a free market, *someone else will step in to provide the product.* Free markets do that.

Because of the positive relationship between price and quantity in the law of supply, the supply curve has a positive slope. Look to the graph below:

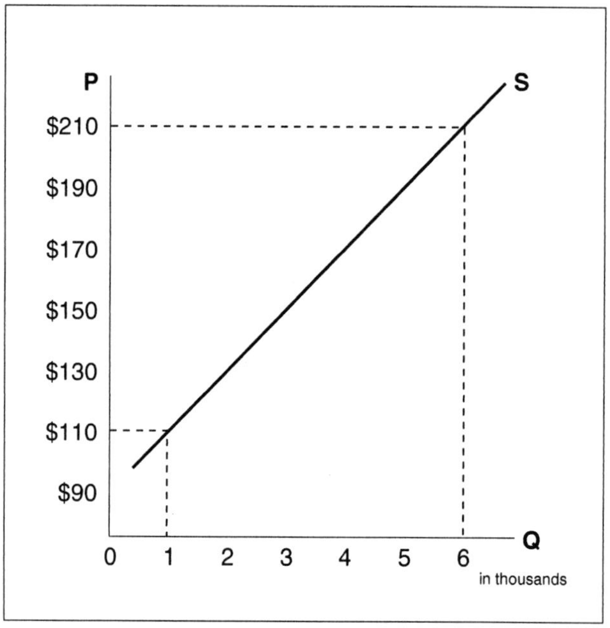

At $110, a producer would choose to make only 1,000 of the item. However, if for some reason, the price rises to $210, the law of supply states that more product will be made and supplied to the market.

The Pressing Question

10. Draw a supply curve graph. Then add a demand curve. Be sure to label everything.

J. Elasticity of Supply

Changes in the price offered by the market will affect the amount of goods produced by businesses. The degree to which a product's supply is impacted by price is called the **elasticity of supply**. The issue is not one of choice. If the price that consumers are offering for a product goes up, producers would be foolish not to make more. However, can they make more? The key phrase to remember in this tricky area of economics is **ease of production.**

Let's compare two different products. On one hand, a factory that makes tie-dyed T-shirts responds to higher prices by a massive increase in production. The shirts are relatively cheap and easy to make. We could say that they have an elastic supply. Consider the following graph:

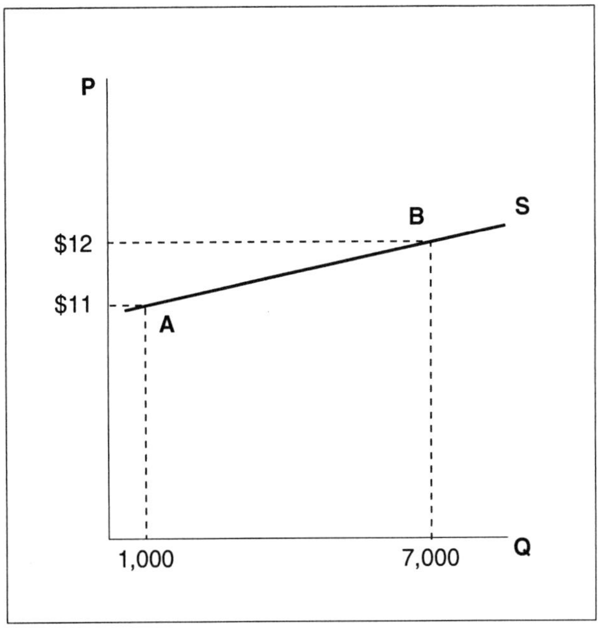

Notice how the supply curve allows the Q to stretch from point A to point B with a very small increase in price. That stretchiness is why T-shirts are considered a product with an elastic supply.

On the other hand, let's consider the Boeing 777. A third-world dictator wishes to pay double sticker price to build an airline for his country. He is angered to learn that Boeing turns down his offer to buy twenty planes at $300 million each, especially when they only cost $150 million to begin with. Go back to the ease of production phrase that was mentioned earlier. Jets are not something you whip up during an all-nighter. They are massive pieces of intricate machinery and technology. No matter what you offer, Boeing simply cannot make an abundance of them. See if that makes sense as you look at the situation graphed below:

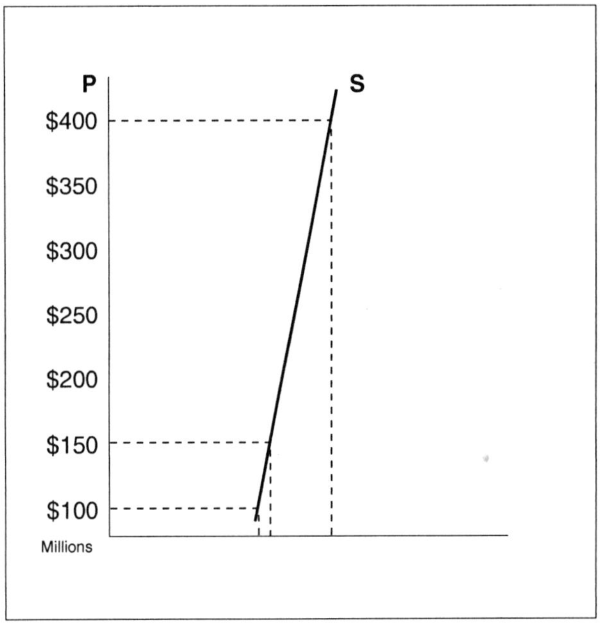

The quantity does not stretch very much from left to right. Hence, economists refer to a product like jets as having an **inelastic supply**.

The Pressing Question

11. List three other products that you think are inelastic in their supply. Explain why.

K. Supply Curves Move When Supply Increases or Decreases

Even if price remains constant, other factors may force supply to increase or decrease. Businesses are often faced with many obstacles in getting products to the marketplace. These factors are called **determinants of supply**. There are four:

- **Technological improvement**—If Ford buys new robots to work in its factories, productivity will increase. More Fords will hit the marketplace even if prices have remained constant.
- **Resource prices**—The price of resources or factors usually refers to anything needed to make a product or provide a service. If a steel shortage causes production problems at Caterpillar, the amount of tractors the company will be able to make may decrease.
- **Taxes and subsidies**—While you should know what a tax is, a **subsidy** is a monetary grant to a business to help ease production or develop a new product. Taxes add to production costs and will result in lower supplies at a given price. If more money is coming in the form of subsidy, costs will decrease and result in higher supplies.
- **Competition**—When in-line skates started to become popular, there were only a few companies in the field. As the popularity became evident to business people, more producers entered the market. Prices remained competitive, but the supplies and choices of in-line skates swelled.

Examine the following graph, and try to choose which line indicates an increase in supply and which one shows a decrease:

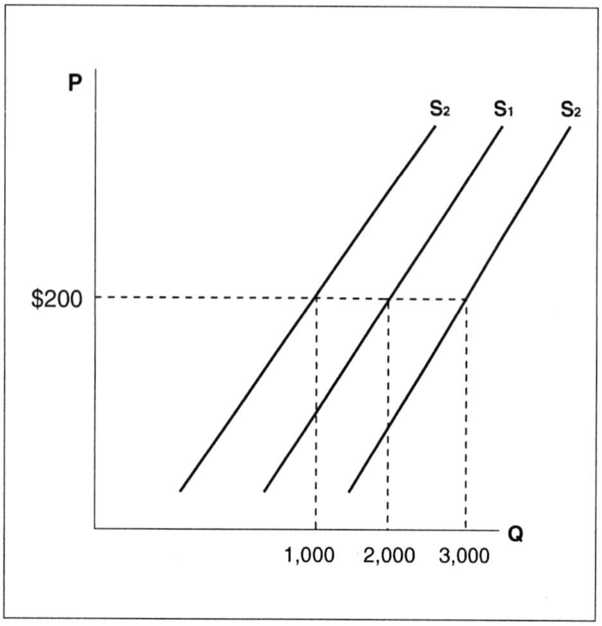

The Pressing Question

12. The product is Boeing 777s. For each of the four determinants of supply, think of a situation that would increase the supply of planes.

L. Supply and Demand Meet at Last

The price system is the means by which the price of a good or service is determined in a pure market economy. When a business produces something, it hopes to find a customer, retrieve the money spent in production, and hopefully make a profit. When a business approaches the marketplace, it posts a price that says to customers "if you want my product, you'll have to give me this much."

Consumers also approach the market with something to say. If they choose to buy, they confirm to the business that they consider the price fair. If they pass, the producer is being told that the price is not acceptable. The business will respond by lowering prices until people start to buy.

As you may have guessed, price is determined graphically at the point where the supply and demand curves meet. This point is often called **equilibrium**. It occurs when the supply for a product matches the demand for a product. While this is an ideally stable market situation, it is rarely static.

Find the price and quantity at the equilibrium point on the following graph:

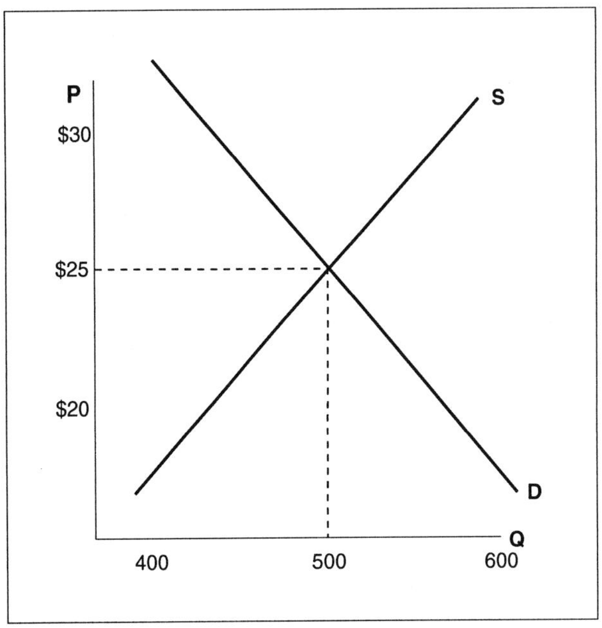

The Pressing Question

13. a. What is the current equilibrium price of gasoline? of cafeteria pizza?

b. In the space below, draw supply and demand graphs that show the price you indicated.

M. Shortages and Surpluses

Businesses are constantly challenged to find out exactly what price to charge consumers. Furthermore, they must try to gauge how much of their product the consumer will be willing to buy. Because of this uncertainty, markets are rarely docile, as the price system fluctuates to find a true resting point.

The problems are easiest to understand in an example. The computer industry decides to produce 400,000 laptops at a price of $1,200 apiece. The processors are very fast, and the accessories are very appealing to the public. Because of the competitive price, the sales are very brisk. Orders pour in from around the country for an astonishing 800,000 computers. The market is met with a **shortage**. In other words, the quantity demanded exceeded the quantity supplied at the given price. Inspect the graph that follows:

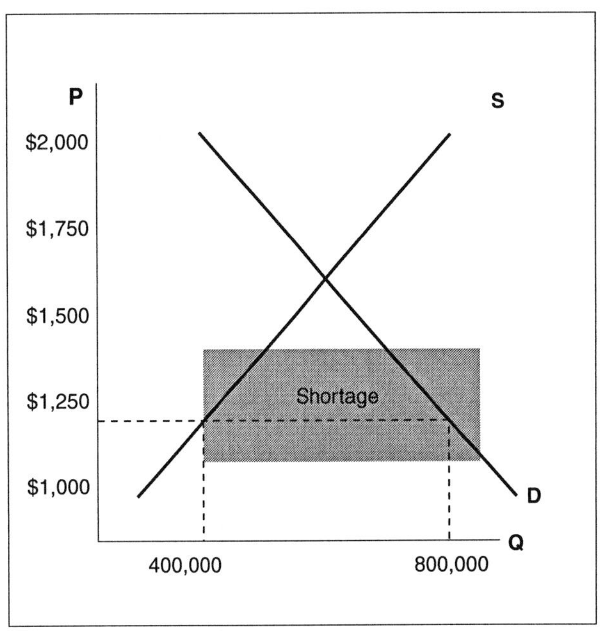

Notice that the $1,200 price is too low for this market. The various companies decide to raise the price of the computer to decrease the consumer demand and to maximize their profits. The price will be raised until a proper equilibrium point is reached.

On the other hand, a **surplus** is when the demand does not meet quantity supplied. Here is a good example. The same industry decides to produce 400,000 laptops and charge $2,000 per unit. At that price, sales are sluggish, and consumers decide to buy from other companies. Management notices that there are thousands of computers in the warehouse. Looking at the graph on the previous page again, see if you can spot the reason for the surplus.

At that price, customers balked. The company is forced to lower the price to increase the amount of sales. They will drop the price until the computers sell more briskly. The matter is urgent because the company cannot afford to have the machines become outdated. Businesses have bills to pay too!

The Pressing Question

14. Recall a recent sale that you've heard of on a big screen TV, stereo, or computer. What were the initial prices versus the sale prices? Was the store suffering from a surplus or shortage?

N. Floors and Ceilings

After World War II, many veterans came home and immediately decided to start families. Because of this, there was a great demand for housing in American cities. Some local governments decided to impose rent control on apartments. In other words, according to their own beliefs, they believed that prices were too high and decided to set a maximum price that landlords could charge. We call that a *price ceiling*. See if you can notice the problem that arises when rent controls are imposed on the graph below:

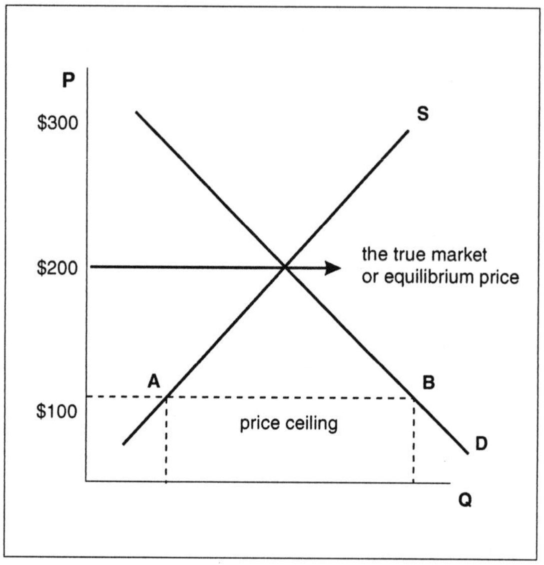

At point A, the supply of apartments will be very low as landlords rebel against the law and realize that they cannot afford to rent at that low price. The demand that you can see at point B is very high. Because of the low price, everyone wants to rent. But the shortage will leave many people without a place to live.

On the other hand, some American prices are set by government price controls. Imagine that unions appeal to the government for higher wages to keep up with cost of living increases. Because it believes that the minimum wage is too low, the government will set a higher one. Notice the graph below:

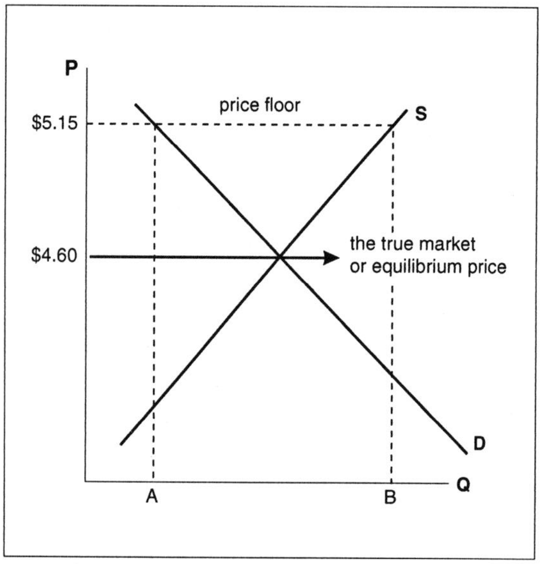

The equilibrium price is too low according to the unions, workers, and the government. They set a new price that is higher than the market wants. At point A, notice that the quantity demanded is very low. On the other hand, at point B, there will be too many workers for the available jobs. This will result in a surplus.

To sum up, whenever they are effective, price floors will usually result in a surplus, and price ceilings will usually result in shortages. Note that they can be ineffective if the ceiling price is set above the equilibrium price or if the floor price is set below the equilibrium price.

The Pressing Question

15. Reread the last sentence. If the government wants to use a price ceiling on a product, what advice would you give?

O. Price and Quantity Change When Supply and Demand Shift

When you read about the different determinants of supply and demand, it probably seemed a bit confusing that a curve would shift from left to right. Hopefully, this section will shed some light on why those shifts are so important. You see, when the curves move for whatever reason, the equilibrium point will end up in a new location.

Decreasing Supply

If there is a shortage of steel, the auto industry will have to alter its production levels. If the auto industry chooses to cut production according to the availability of steel, the amount of cars produced will go down. Consider the following graph:

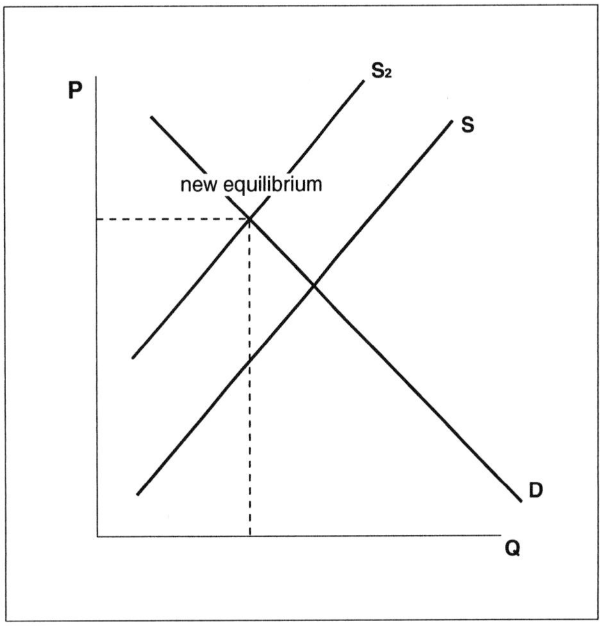

The supply of cars decreased because of a severe steel shortage and the material has become more scarce. Logically, the company will have to produce less cars to maintain the same price. The quantity must move left on the x-axis as the curve shifts to the left. Notice the new equilibrium indicates a higher price with a lower quantity. Consumers will have to pay more for cars if they want them. Remember, whenever the supply or demand curve moves, a **new equilibrium** will be created. In the case above, a decrease in the supply will create a higher price. Keep in mind that both curves can move, and they can move in either direction. In any situation, equilibrium will end up in a new place.

Increasing Demand

Notice the different situation that follows:

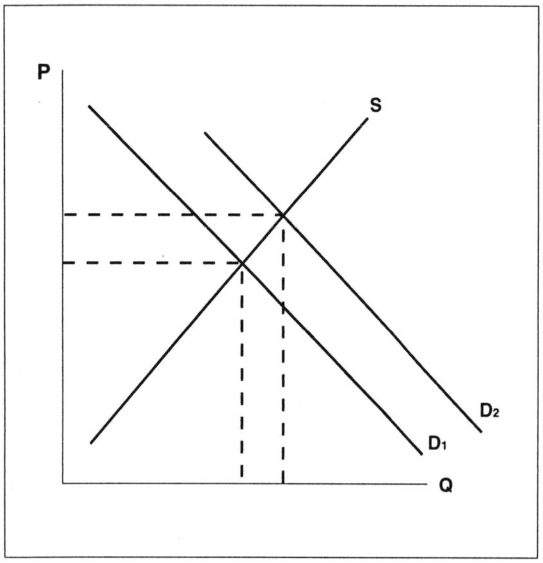

The graph represents the supply and demand for CDs. This band became more popular, and so demand increased substantially. The quantity increased as did the price. The determinant of consumer tastes and preferences will cause movement in a demand curve. The market for that particular CD will have a higher price and a higher amount sold.

Music stores are constantly trying to figure out how the likes and dislikes of teenagers will impact the demand for recorded popular music. CDs that were once popular may now be priced too high, leaving the store with a surplus. They will need to drop their prices (have a sale) to move the remainder of their merchandise.

Increasing Supply

If the government decides to subsidize a certain carmaker's efforts to produce cars, the cost of production for the company will decrease, thus making it easier for the company to make cars. The situation would look like this:

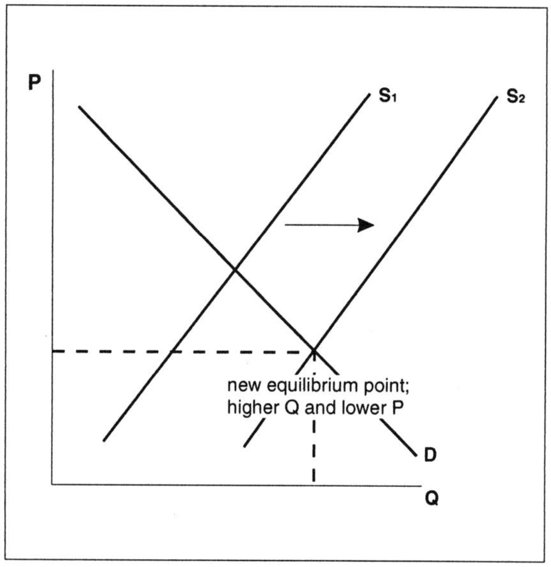

Remember that a **subsidy** is a cash grant that is given to a company to aid the company in the production of a particular good or service. For instance, maybe the government wants Ford to produce electric cars. Because new technology is very costly, the extra money will help defray the expense. This will allow the company to produce more cars at a cheaper price.

Decreasing Demand

What happens if a product suddenly falls out of favor with the public? For instance, baggy pants like those worn by the rapper MC Hammer sold like hotcakes a number of years ago. As his popularity waned, the demand for the pants went down drastically. Look at the graph below.

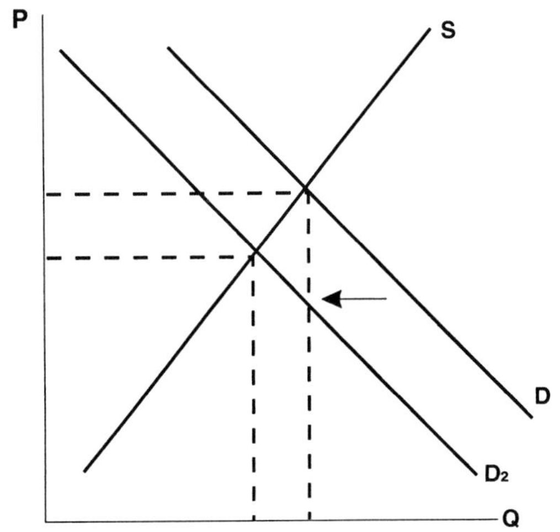

In the end, the curve would move to a point that no matter what the supply, the demand would be zero. As Hammer's popularity decreased, so did the demand for his baggy pants and other merchandise. While that seems like common sense, the ability to show the change graphically will help you figure out complex problems at some point in the future.

Essential Facts to Remember about Curves

1. They are models of reality.
2. They graph what is common sense and will help you to keep more complex situations straight.
3. They are loved by college professors, and if you study business later, you will use them in abundance.
4. Always make sure you label them correctly.
5. They are rarely neat straight lines.

The Pressing Question

16. Create four curves. Follow the instructions below:

    a. Draw the x and y axes.

    b. Mark P and Q.

    c. Draw in and label the S and D curves.

    d. Then make one of them
    - an increasing demand
    - a decreasing supply
    - an increasing supply
    - a decreasing demand

    e. Invent a scenario that explains why the demand or supply shifted in each one.

    f. Indicate where the new equilibrium point is. Use a dotted line to show how price and quantity related.

Name________________________

Date________________________

How Big?

Directions: Find the words that fit the blanks from your reading. Then unscramble the boxed letters to answer the question "How big is our economy?"

1. a system of production and consumption — __ __ [ ] __ __ __ __
2. the study of the distribution of scarce resources — __ __ __ __ __ __ __ __ __
3. the type of economy we have in the United States — __ __ __ [ ] __
4. an economic system in which the factors of production are held in private hands — __ __ __ __ __ __ [ ] __ __ __
5. a good that is commonly used in conjunction with another good — __ __ __ __ __ __ __ __ __ __
6. a market in which supply cannot meet the demand — __ [ ] __ __ __ __ [ ] __
7. a good that is commonly used to replace another good — __ __ __ __ __ __ __ __ __ __
8. People try to satisfy their wants and ________. — __ __ __ __ __
9. The price of making an economic decision is called ______ cost. — __ __ __ __ __ __ __ __ __ __ __
10. a maximum price set for a product — __ __ [ ] __ __ __ __
11. a person who risks capital to start a new business venture — __ __ __ [ ] __ __ __ __ __ __ __ __
12. another word for money or things bought with money — __ [ ] __ __ __ __ __
13. Supply exceeds the demand for a product. — __ [ ] __ __ __ __ __
14. the human element in the process of production — __ __ __ [ ] __
15. new methods and innovations of production — __ __ __ __ [ ] __ __ __ __ __

Name________________________

Date________________________

16. the usefulness or satisfaction one gets from using a product — ___ ___ ___ ___ ___ ___ ___

17. the study of economics on a smaller scale — ___ ___ ___ ___ ___ ☐ ___ ___ ___ ___ ___ ___ ___ ___

18. the relationship between price and quantity — ___ ___ ___ ☐ ___ ___ ___ ___ ___ ___

19. a minimum price set for a product — ___ ___ ☐ ___ ___

20. When price goes up, quantity goes down. This is the law of ____. — ___ ☐ ☐ ___ ___ ___

21. When price goes up, quantity goes up. This is the law of _____. — ___ ___ ___ ___ ___ ___

22. a type of economy in which customs decide who gets what and why — ___ ☐ ___ ___ ___ ___ ___ ___ ___ ___ ___

How big is our economy?

___ ___ ___ ___ c ___ ___ ___ ___ y ___ ___ ___ e ___ l ___ y ___ u ___ ___.

Name____________________________

Date____________________________

The Factors of Production

Part A.

Directions: Choose five products or services, and fill in the chart with each of the factors of production needed to manufacture or provide them.

Product	Labor	Natural Resources	Entrepreneur	Capital
1.				
2.				
3.				
4.				
5.				

Part B.

Directions: Wherever and whenever you go in the world, people consume and produce the things they want and need. For each of the following economies, consult **Handout 1** to get appropriate examples and then specify who makes the decisions of production and consumption.

Economy	Example	Who decides who gets what and why?
Traditional		
Command		
Market		
Socialist		
Mixed		

Name________________________

Date________________________

Our Economy in Operation

Directions: Thoroughly answer the following questions. Be prepared for class discussion.

1. People say that our economy is doing well right now. What does that mean?

2. a. What prevents a stranger from entering your home and taking your possessions?

   b. What rights of yours are being violated by such an intruder?

3. Name five ways that our government is involved with our economy.

4. If the economy gets bad, list five negative impacts that we would notice.

5. What is utility, and how does it relate to pizza? How do you know that?

6. What do you suppose are the three most important ways to keep track of the economy?

Name____________________________

Date____________________________

7. Consider the pictures below. Create a time line of the two-hundred-year life span of the United States that details some of the major economic and technological innovations of our history. Provide some descriptions of changing technology, labor, and demographics.

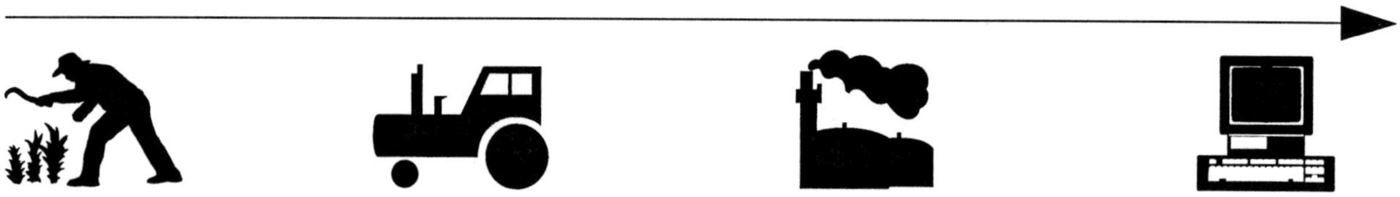

8. Who protects our economic rights?

9. What makes our standard of living higher than other countries? How does the economy impact your standard of living?

Fundamentals of Economics
Lesson 4
Handout 5

Name______________________

Date______________________

Graphing Supply and Demand

Directions: Complete the following tables and graph.

Below are two schedules representing the supply and demand for cheeseburgers in your school cafeteria. The prices are provided. In the quantity columns, fill in figures that you think would be appropriate. One figure is filled in to get you started.

Demand

Price	Quantity
$0.25	________
$0.50	________
$0.75	________
$1.00	150
$1.25	________
$1.50	________

(what the market is willing to buy at a given price)

Supply (Remember that Q will fall as P falls.)

Price	Quantity
$0.25	________
$0.50	________
$0.75	________
$1.00	150
$1.25	________
$1.50	________

(what the market is willing to buy at a given price)

For the figures that you calculated above, label and fill in the graph below. (Don't forget to label P and Q.)

Name__________________________

Date___________________________

Graphing Problems

Directions: For each scenario, complete the following steps. Indicate whether supply or demand is being changed on the product in parentheses.

- Write down the correct determinant.
- Label the graph given.
- Draw in the new supply or demand curve.
- Using a dotted line, show the new equilibrium point.
- Indicate what happened to the price and quantity of the product.

Example

The size of your school doubles. __*D*____ (cafeteria pizza)

Determinant __*size of market*__

P goes up

Q goes up

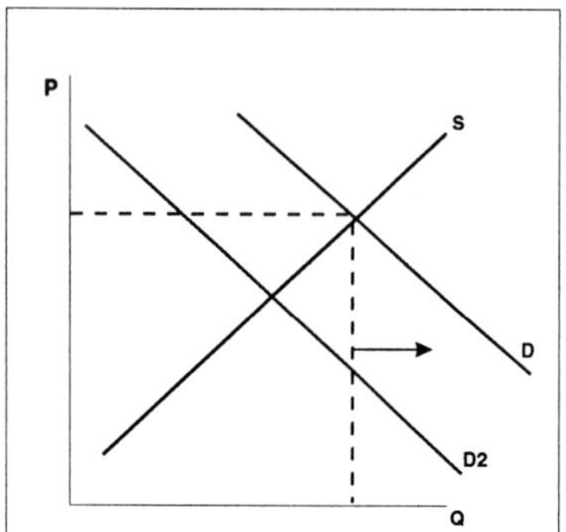

Cafeteria pizza

1. There is a sale on hamburgers one day. ____________________ (cafeteria pizza)

Determinant __________________

Name__________________________

Date___________________________

2. Reebok becomes the official footwear provider of all NBA players. ____________________ (Nike)

   Determinant ____________________

3. There is a steel shortage in the United States. ____________________ (cars)

   Determinant ____________________

4. A government imposes a stiff emissions tax on a factory. ____________________ (Fords)

   Determinant ____________________

Name___________________________

Date___________________________

5. New automated robots are bought to make the pizza. _______________ (pizza in the cafeteria)

   Determinant _______________

6. Coke cuts its prices in half. _______________ (Pepsi)

   Determinant _______________

7. Eight new companies join the bike market. _______________ (mountain bikes)

   Determinant _______________

Name____________________

Date____________________

8. New manufacturing methods cut production prices in half. ________________ (computers)

   Determinant ________________

9. The United States experiences a baby boom. ________________ (diapers)

   Determinant ________________

10. The price of potatoes falls by 300 percent. ________________ (french fries)

    Determinant ________________

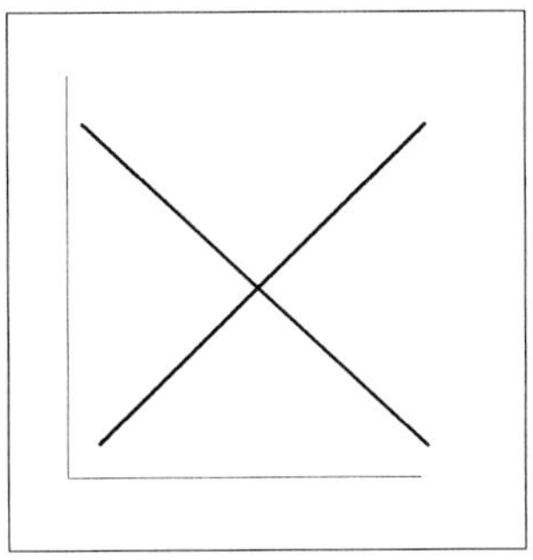

Name__________________________

Date___________________________

11. The U.S. government promises a $2 billion subsidy. ________________ (GM's new electric car)

    Determinant __________________

12. There are massive jelly shortages due to bad fruit crops as prices climb.
    __________________ (peanut butter)

    Determinant __________________

13. Consumers fear that there will be a recession in the near future.
    __________________ (gasoline)

    Determinant __________________

Name________________________

Date________________________

Thought Questions

Directions: For each of the following questions, provide answers with the help of your book, outside sources, or adults. Write your answers in complete sentences.

1. An economy is defined as "a system of producing and consuming." What could happen if there is too much consuming for the stuff that is produced?

2. If consumers don't consume all that is produced, what happens then?

3. How do we know if we are experiencing a bad economy? Give an example.

4. When VCRs first appeared in the late 1970s, they cost thousands of dollars. If they are so high-tech, how did they get so affordable in the last few years?

5. What new technologies radically transformed our economy in the 1800s?

6. What new technologies are radically transforming our economy now?

Name__________________________

Date___________________________

7. In 1800, the United States was an agricultural/rural society. What are we today?

8. What benefits come from having a very productive society?

9. What technologies have faded in your lifetime?

10. Where does the United States stand in the world economically?

11. How is the job market changing because of our changing economy?

12. If we have so much money, why are there still poor people in the United States?

13. How does capitalism (free market) keep our economy moving?

Part 2
Business and Labor

Questions to Consider

1. How does a business make money?
2. How do you calculate a company's worth?
3. What are the differences between big and small businesses?
4. Are there different types of businesses?
5. How do we deal with monopolies if they still exist?
6. In what ways do businesses deal with their workers?
7. How do unions affect our overall economy?
8. What sorts of jobs are going to be out there in the next twenty years?

Terms You Need in Order to Read

Corporation	Perfect competition	Strike
Profit	Merger	Wages
Productivity	Union	

Name______________________

Date______________________

Business and Labor

Directions: Read the selection, and answer the Pressing Questions as you read. Be prepared for class discussion.

A. Starting a Business

If you have already held a job in your lifetime, chances are you worked for a business. Think about the nature of that business. In other words:

- What does the business provide?
- Who owns it?
- How much money do you think it makes a year?
- What are its operating costs?

Just thinking about it for a minute can help you gain a new level of respect for the owners of that business. Starting a business can be extraordinarily difficult. Businesses are expensive, risky, and time-consuming. On the other hand, the satisfaction that comes from engineering a successful venture is quite rewarding.

Most people at some point dream of owning their own business. Perhaps they believe they have found a niche in the marketplace that has not yet been tapped. Maybe they think that they have invented a device that could be useful to consumers or to industry. Sometimes the reason is even simpler: they want to be their own boss.

Paul is such a person. He has been a landscaper for five years. He understands the business and sees the potential for profit. His company charges seventy dollars per hour to cut and maintain lawns. Many times, even the big lawns only take an hour to cut in the first place. His company pays him and his coworkers a combined thirty dollars an hour. He often sits down and figures out what sort of profits he could make if he were the owner of the business.

At lunch, he looks at the pickup truck and trailer containing all of their equipment. To start his business, he estimates he would need about twenty thousand dollars to buy all of the items necessary to begin. Paul decides to seek out what is known as **venture capital.** This is money that is invested in new businesses with a considerable amount of risk. The bank was not willing to lend Paul the money because of the high risk involved. Secondly, Paul lacked sufficient **collateral,** anything of value that can be used as a guarantee that the loan will be repaid. Banks, as you will learn, are very cautious when they lend their money. Rarely do they lend money to people based upon their good name. They need to be assured that the money will be paid back in a timely fashion.

Leaving the bank, Paul resolves to find the money somewhere else. His determination takes him to a friend who had recently inherited some money. Paul proposes to combine his own resources with his friend's to buy a truck, equipment, and some business insurance. It is now up to Paul to find customers, a few reliable employees, and the energy to make it all work.

The Pressing Question

1. Paul formed a business with a combination of his friend's capital and his own savings. What sort of business are they agreeing to form? How should they handle the distribution of the profits?

B. Two Types of Smaller Businesses

There are five main types of businesses in the American marketplace. Each one is structured to best suit its function, owner, and product. While each type will have certain restrictions and disadvantages, each will also have specific rewards to those who are lucky enough to own them.

A **sole proprietorship** is a business owned and controlled by one person. This is the most common business found in the United States today. But because of the financial constraints placed on one person, sole proprietorships are often small "mom and pop" establishments. Also, many doctors, skilled craftsmen, insurance firms, real estate firms, lawyers, beauticians, and bakers are in business on their own.

The greatest advantages to a small, owner-run business is the small amount of money needed to start it. Also, no complicated arrangements or forms need to be filed with the state. While even the smallest of businesses must comply with local zoning restrictions, they will also have to acquire any appropriate licenses from the city or county in which they operate. For example, in many places, any establishment that sells alcohol must have a liquor license from the local government.

Some sole proprietors consider the autonomy they have over their own work-lives to be the greatest reward to running a small business. They are their own boss. Even better, the profits of the business go nowhere but into their own pockets. Many are motivated by the personal satisfaction that comes from the promises of success. The heart of an entrepreneur thrives on the chance of great profit, personal satisfaction, prestige, and psychological rewards.

On the other side of sole proprietorships, some disadvantages must be considered. The lack of capital can stunt the growth of a successful business. Many times, a lot of money must be borrowed. Then, financial **liability** can be quite daunting. Included with this problem is any debt owed by the business. Personal assets comprise much of the money used to start small businesses. If bills get too great, creditors may seek to possess the owner's personal assets. The business and owner are legally considered one entity. Moreover, if the business causes injury or damage to someone or something, the victim may seek compensation in the form of the owner's personal holdings. These holdings often include houses and life savings. As you can see, there is so much at stake for the small business owner.

Many streets around our country look like this. Small businesses do not account for most of the country's GDP, but they greatly outnumber larger corporations.

To alleviate some of the hassles in starting a sole proprietorship, many people decide to form partnerships. A **partnership** is a business that is owned and controlled by two or more people. By nature, partnerships are usually small and require smaller amounts of money to get started. The most common are businesses that offer professional services like lawyers, accountants, and doctors.

The most important feature in a partnership is the partnership contract that clearly states the liability and responsibility of each owner. In the contract, each owner will be specified as a general partner or limited partner. A **general partner** has equal say in the decisions of the business but shares in the liability. **Limited partners** avoid losing personal assets, but they sacrifice some of their decision-making power. Limited partnerships in other countries are often noted in the name of the business by the *Ltd.* that follows the business' name.

Partnerships offer many advantages. First, they can offer the same personal satisfaction as a sole proprietorship. Second, partnerships require relatively little capital and are relatively simple to form. They can also become more efficient when the owners share the responsibility that is appropriate to their specific skill. For example, in a law firm, one partner can manage divorce cases, another can do only bankruptcy cases, and a third may be the managing partner who handles all the expenses of operation. Decisions can be made easier by pooling each other's knowledge. Lastly, liability and losses of a partnership are lessened because they are divided evenly or according to the partnership contract.

There are some disadvantages to consider. Both general and limited partners are subject to some sort of liability, but general partners put their personal assets at risk. Another obvious problem that may arise are personal disagreements. Pooled knowledge may help the growth of a business, but personalities might clash as well. This problem may seem minor, but when there is money at stake, problems usually find a way to surface.

The Pressing Question

2. Propose three ideas for a small business you think could someday make it big.

C. Types of Corporations

Paul's small landscaping business has grown considerably in the last few years. To get to a higher level in this occupation, Paul needs to buy a fleet of trucks, a warehouse, and lots of equipment. He estimates that the investment will cost close to $200,000. Based upon the past success of the business, many people in the area have voiced their interest in joining the business with Paul. If they do decide to invest, they will want to own part of the business. This will thus entitle them to a share of the profits that Paul makes.

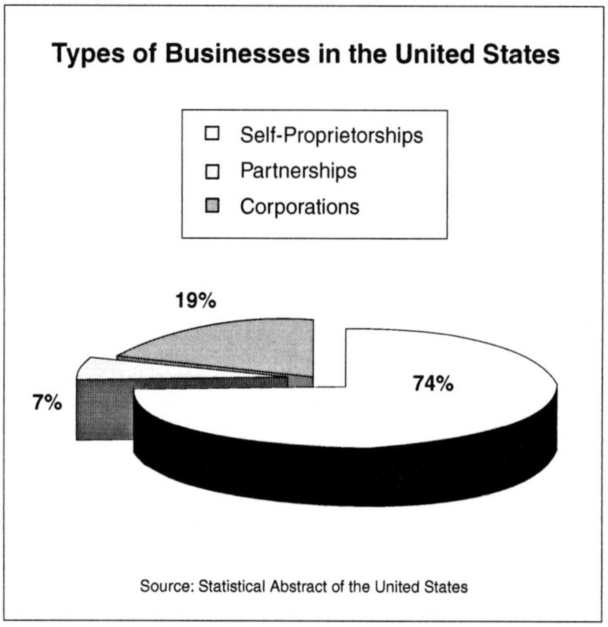

Paul decides to forfeit part of the company in order to raise the capital for expansion. He issues 400,000 shares of **stock**, or certificates that grant the holder to a piece of a company. He will keep 300,000 for himself and sell the

Top 25 Public Corporations According to Sales, 2000

Rank	Company	Sales (in millions)	Employees (in thousands)
1	General Motors	176,558	392.0
2	Wal-Mart Stores	165,013	*
3	Ford Motor	162,558	364.6
4	Exxon Mobil	160,883	115.0
5	General Electric	111,630	316.5
6	International Business Machines	87,548	299.2
7	Citigroup	82,005	173.5
8	AT&T	62,391	141.1
9	Philip Morris Cos	61,751	0.0
10	Boeing	57,993	211.0
11	Bank of America	51,632	163.4
12	SBC Communications	49,489	202.5
13	Kroger	45,352	300.0
14	Hewlett-Packard	43,808	84.4
15	Sears, Roebuck	41,071	324.0
16	American International Group	40,656	52.3
17	Enron	40,112	17.9
18	Procter & Gamble	39,118	108.2
19	Compaq Computer	38,525	69.1
20	Lucent Technologies	38,467	153.0
21	Home Depot	38,434	156.2
22	Albertson's	37,478	220.0
23	MCI WorldCom	37,120	77.3
24	Fannie Mae	36,969	3.9
25	Kmart	35,925	278.5

Reprinted by Permission of *Forbes Magazine* © 2000 Forbes.

Top 12 U.S. Corporations Ranked by Profit, 2000

Rank	Company	Profits (in billions)
1	General Electric	10,717
2	Citigroup	9,994
3	Microsoft	8,746
4	Exxon Mobil	7,910
5	Bank of America	7,882
6	International Business Machines	7,712
7	EI du Pont de Nemours	7,690
8	Philip Morris Cos	7,675
9	Intel	7,314
10	Ford Motor	7,236
11	SBC Communications	6,573
12	General Motors	6,002

Reprinted by Permission of *Forbes Magazine* © 2000 Forbes.

While General Motors leads the country in sales, it is twelfth in profits. Why?

remaining 100,000 to investors at $2 per share. Because Paul chooses whom to sell stock to and does not sell on the open market, this arrangement is known as closed or **private corporation**. In the future, the company may choose to sell more stock to raise more money on a public stock exchange. It will then become a **public corporation**. At this point, however, Paul owns 75 percent of the company and the various investors own 25 percent. The profits are divided accordingly, and the new owners will have some say in the direction of the company.

So Paul raised the $200,000 needed to expand. The results were record profits. But because he sacrificed some of the ownership, he will only get 75 percent of the profits. Imagine that the company made one million dollars in the first year. The profits should be divided evenly according to the amount of shares in the company.

$1,000,000 / 400,000 shares = $2.50

For each share of stock owned, the holder will get a dividend, or share of the profits, of $2.50. However, the owners of the business may decide to keep some of the money in the company for future expansion or a capital reserve. While the dividends for the year will be smaller, the business will have more potential for success. This practice in known as **internal financing**.

Forming a corporation can be complicated. When Paul set out to incorporate his business, he consulted a corporate lawyer. It was then he learned about the many legal restrictions involved with such business arrangements. The lawyer filled out an application with the State of Ohio for a **corporate charter**. This is a license that states the business' location, ownership, and length of existence. It also gives a business the right to operate as a corporation. In other words, Paul's business will be regarded by the law as an individual. For example, if the someone wishes to sue the business, they will sue the corporation and not Paul. They can never go after his personal assets.

In the original company charter of Paul Landscaping Co., Paul was named Chief Executive Officer. Officers of companies usually make the day-to-day decisions of how the corporation is run. Paul also has a seat on the fourteen-member Board of Directors. These people will include the other major stockholders and a collection of other knowledgeable people who can aid in the larger decisions of the company. After the officers, there may be directors and managers.

The major advantage of a corporation is the lack of liability created by stockholders' separation of ownership. If the business fails, the investor can lose only the amount of the original investment. Furthermore, if the business is sued, stockholders are free from losing their personal assets and property. Secondly, stockholders can invest in companies that they know nothing about while experts in what the company produces deal with all management issues. Stockholders may earn big profits while doing no work! Or they may also lose a lot without any input into the decisions of the corporation.

Corporations also have easier access to capital than partnerships and sole proprietorships. If the management decides to expand, they can sell stock or borrow money from investors or banks. Many large corporations are constantly borrowing money for day-to-day operations, product development, or modernization.

Despite the advantages, there are some drawbacks to corporations. They are often slow to make decisions because of the many people involved in the running of the company. Proposals must run through a complicated chain of command where disagreements may arise. Second, the corporation must pay a tax on its profits before it pays the dividends to stockholders. Once received, the shareholders must pay a **tax** on the dividends as well. This is a dilemma known as **double taxation**. Furthermore, if the value of the stock goes up, the investor must pay a **capital gains tax** on the money made.

Despite the disadvantages, millions of people invest in corporations every year. Furthermore, while corporations comprise only 20 percent of the businesses in the United States, they account for over 90 percent of the total sales in the country. In fact, many of our top companies produce more goods in a year than many less developed countries.

The Pressing Questions

3. The previous section states that the Board of Directors makes the big decisions of many corporations. What do you suppose are three of the biggest decisions a corporation makes every year?

4. If you wanted to know the value of a share of IBM stock, where could you look to find out?

5. If you decided to invest in IBM, where could you go to do it?

D. Other Types of Businesses

One inviting way to start a business is to buy a **franchise**, which is a contractual agreement that allows a parent company to sell the use of its name and merchandise to an independent businessperson. For example, if you wanted to have your own McDonald's restaurant, you would have to enter into a franchise agreement. This would state that for a fee, you would attain access to the know-how and products associated with the golden arches. On the other hand, you would have to run your **franchise** according to their established company policies.

When you get to college, you may have the option of joining a book **cooperative**. A co-op, as they are called, is a business that is owned by the people who use its services. Students buy a share of the cooperative, and in turn, they get the books they need at reduced prices. The concept is used in various ways:

- Credit unions have people pool their savings together so that money can be borrowed by fellow members at lower interest rates when needed.
- Marketing co-ops take products of many producers and sell them under one name. In this way, members will save on advertising costs and packaging.
- Housing co-ops are corporations formed by people who occupy a common building or land. This helps them share the risk and cost of maintaining the property.
- Service cooperatives like the Council of Smaller Enterprises (COSE) pool their need for services together to bring the cost of services down for their members.

The last type of business that operates in the United States is known as a **nonprofit.** These businesses offer goods and services without seeking a profit. Any excess money generated gets put back into the organization. Charities like the Red Cross, American Heart Association, and the Girl Scouts are only a few of the more common nonprofits. Revenues come from selling of products and services, and contributions from benefactors.

United Way®

The Pressing Question

6. List five nonprofit organizations that you know about.

E. Common Problems Faced by Businesses

Just like individuals, businesses have to face a myriad of trade-offs when they make an economic decision. Each of these decisions will have some sort of opportunity cost. For example, if Taylor Shoes Inc. decides to put a factory in a major city, they will have the added benefit of being close to a lot of major highways and railroad depots. However, they will not be able to take advantage of the lower taxes offered by the local suburbs. Each decision has to be weighed carefully and considered.

One of the toughest decisions is trying to figure out how much of a product to produce. This decision can be made easier by a **production possibilities curve**. Assuming that all variables like resource availability and technology stay the same during a given time period, the curve can be a useful tool in the production process.

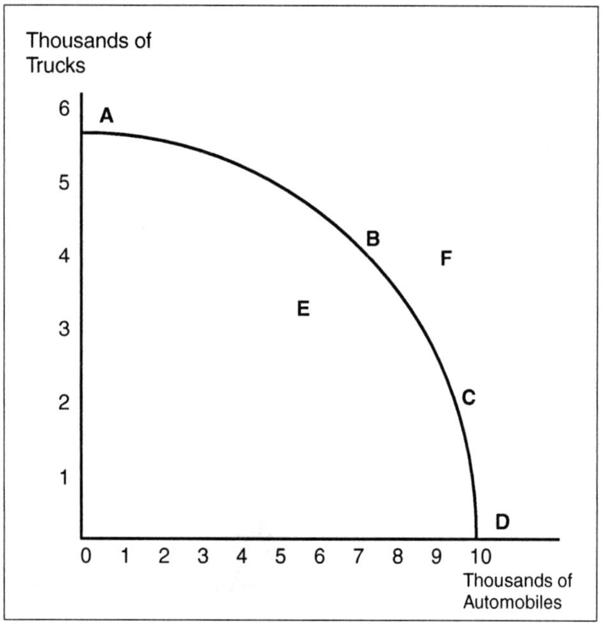

The curve shows the different amounts of two products can be produced. If you choose to produce 5,300 trucks, no cars can be made. On the other hand, if 10,000 cars are made, no trucks can be produced. More importantly, if the production combination falls within the field, it means that the resources of the company are not being use to maximum efficiency (point E). The managers will scramble to figure out how to make the company more productive.

Keep in mind that the production possibilities curve is simply a model of reality. These models used in economics can show us problems like low productivity. If the company is not performing up to expectations according to the model, they might find the problem and boost profits in the long run. It can also show what could happen in the future. A business might set a goal like located at point F. If all goes well, in the next several months, the company may hit point F. Remember though, at this given time, F is not attainable, given the current resources and technology.

The main function of the production possibilities curve is to show that if you produce a certain amount of one product, you can only produce a certain amount of the other. If you choose to produce at point B, you can make 4,000 trucks and 7,000 cars. Remember the basic lesson of economics, if you choose one possibility, it means that it is at the expense of other choices.

A second problem faced by business is called the **law of diminishing returns**. This states that as one resource is added to a fixed supply of other resources during the production process, output or production may increase for a time. Eventually, if the resource is added continually, marginal output will diminish.

For example, if a T-shirt manufacturer hires a new worker, the business will increase production levels. So the manager hires another worker. She sees that the output went up some more. With the third worker, as long as no more machinery or other resources are changed, the output will begin to go down (or the increases will decrease in size). In essence, more is not necessarily better. It is up to a good manager to figure out where the most profitable point lies.

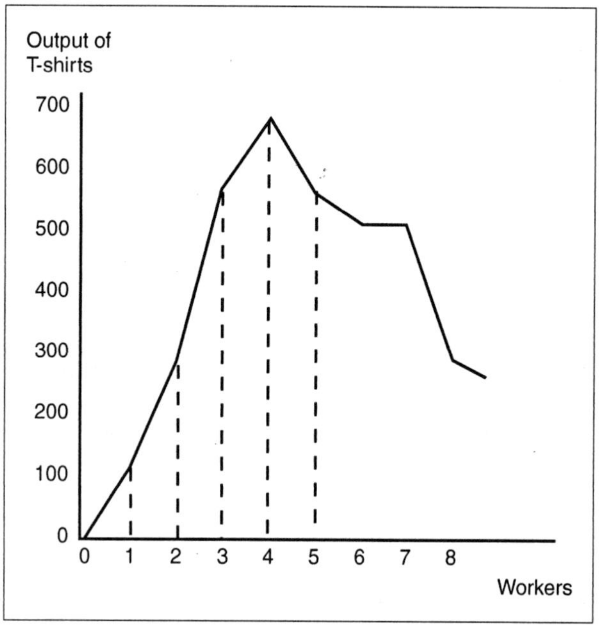

Businesses must also keep an eye on costs. If the name of the game is all about profits, there is a basic formula that you should remember.

Gross Revenue	(P x Q)
- Costs	
Net Revenue	(profits)

When it comes to controlling costs, the more specific a business gets, the better. Costs are often broken down into categories. The most important of these are as follows:

- **Fixed Costs**—These do not vary with output levels. If the output is at 0, these still will have to be paid. These include rent, insurance, debt, and property tax payments. Depreciation, or the aging of capital goods like buildings and machines, is included. Fixed costs are also known as *overhead.*
- **Variable Costs**—These costs change with a change in production level. Raw materials and labor can vary from month to month. Workers can be hired or laid off as needed. Shortages and surpluses can make resource costs move up and down.
- **Total Costs**—The sum of the fixed and variable costs. When the output is zero, the total costs equal the fixed costs.
- **Total Costs Per Unit**—This is simply the total costs divided by the number of units produced.
- **Marginal Costs**—This is the cost of producing one more unit. Businesses watch this figure most closely. They can increase profitability of their product by increasing or decreasing output slightly.

If a business wishes to succeed, these costs must be watched carefully. It is a simple rule. When costs are lower, the profits will increase. A good business will make more product at a lower total cost per unit year after year. Thus, profits will go up. Their **profit margin** is watched closely as well. It is calculated by dividing the revenues by the amount of total sales.

$$\text{Profit Margin} = \frac{\text{Profit}}{\text{Total Sales}}$$

Last, some businesses must address the issue of permanence. If a product is designed to last forever, customers will have no need to buy more. Makers of designer clothes are constantly updating their lines. Car companies design new models to keep customers coming back.

The Pressing Questions

7. If a company sells putters for $85 and it costs $55 to manufacture them, what is the profit margin?

8. What is an acceptable level of profit?

F. Competition and Market Structure

Economists closely watch how businesses interact with one another. Rivalry occurs when businesses compete for a greater share of the market. Each market has a limited amount of customers at a given time, so competition is vital for a business' survival. The market structure describes how a particular group of businesses compete with one another.

Perfect competition is the most ideal market situation for consumers. Three conditions must be present for it to exist. First, there should be a large number of buyers and sellers. Each seller must account for only a small part of the market and attract enough customers to turn a small profit. Second, entering or exiting a market must be easy. Owners can start a business with little money and little technical knowledge. Third, there must be easy access to information. In other words, prices and descriptions of competing products should be easily found. With these three criteria filled, buyers can choose freely from a myriad of products and make their decision based upon price alone.

Pure monopoly is the exact opposite of perfect competition. Instead of many companies offering a product, only one business offers the product. Even if consumers wanted to take their business elsewhere, there are no substitutes. Furthermore, information is controlled by the monopoly. Many times, a monopoly will advertise to boost the image of the product. For example, diamonds are mostly sold by one company in the world. But because of a skilled advertising campaign, the public has a very positive view of diamonds. Last, it must be virtually impossible to enter the market. Either the monopoly will stand in your way, or the costs are too prohibitive.

Would you believe that the government has determined that certain monopolies are beneficial to our economy? There are four such situations:

- **Natural Monopoly**—In some markets, it is impractical to start a new business. For instance, your gas company may enjoy a monopoly in your area, because it is simply too expensive to dig out the streets and lay new pipe. Therefore, the government gives them the right to operate and regulates their prices closely at the state level. While competition is being introduced in certain areas, states use public utility commissions to regulate rates.
- **Technological Monopoly**—If you invent a new product, you may apply for a patent from the U.S. Patent Office. If it is approved, you will have exclusive rights to produce that item for seventeen years. For example, only Polaroid makes instant cameras, as decided in a 1986 Supreme Court decision on their patent. Also, only Microsoft may make and sell their Windows software. Their products are in an estimated 90 percent of the world's computers.
- **Geographic Monopoly**—When a supplier is very isolated, it will most likely have no competition. While people are quite mobile today, it would not pay to have several similar stores in an area where there are very few people.
- **Governmental Monopoly**—Certain services have been determined to be best controlled by governments. The Post Office is provided for in the Constitution. Your local city government probably controls your water and sewer service. The state is in charge of the maintenance of its highways. These issues will be discussed in detail in Part 4.

The Pressing Question

9. What industry in the United States do you consider to be the closest to perfect competition? Explain your answer.

G. Taking on a Monopoly

In the late 1800s, industrialists combined their companies in efforts to create monopolies or combinations in the oil, steel, meat-packing, and sugar industries These efforts did not go unnoticed by the federal government. The government felt that these mergers and market domination would result in unfair prices for American consumers. The government had to combat a prevailing attitude that the markets should remain free of any interference from governmental authority. This attitude of laissez-faire (a French phrase for "leave it be") dominated the thinking of prominent industrialists.

While some monopolies are considered legal by the government, it was determined in the late 1800s that some monopolies were harmful to the public interest. Congress decided to make it illegal for companies to merge with one another if it meant that the market moved too close to monopoly. They began to pass legislation around the turn of the century. Here are three of the more important laws:

- **Sherman Antitrust Act** (1890)—the true cornerstone of U.S. free trade legislation; prohibited any combination, conspiracy, or contract in the restraint of trade.
- **Clayton Anti-Trust Act** (1914)—strengthened the Sherman Act by prohibiting price discrimination, exclusive contracts, local pricing, and interlocking directorates.
- **Federal Trade Commission Act** (1914)—the act that created the Federal Trade Commission (FTC); it is an agency that investigates charges of unfair trade practices and violations of the law.

If someone has a complaint about a business' behavior, he or she can make a complaint to the FTC, which will then stage an investigation. If there is a case, the antitrust division of the Justice Department will have its lawyers bring a case to federal court. At that time, they will attempt to prove that the company's behavior violated antitrust law in some way.

The Justice Department, headed by the Attorney General, investigates complaints against companies accused of violating antitrust law.

In recent decades, the laws have been stringently enforced. In 1984, AT&T was the largest corporation in the world. It was a natural monopoly that smaller phone companies protested. The Justice Department took AT&T to court and argued that it violated antitrust law to have such a big monopoly in America. The courts agreed and forced AT&T to break itself up into eight local phone companies which the press dubbed the "baby bells."

In the mid to late 1980s, American businesses went through a series of large, high-profile mergers which added to a feeling of pro-business sentiment that permeated the public. Many argued that the Sherman and Clayton Acts were harmful to the public because they prevented **economies of scale**. In other words, larger industries can take advantage of mass production and pass the lower prices onto consumers.

The Pressing Questions

10. In what three ways can a monopoly be bad for the American economy?

11. In what way could a monopoly be good?

H. The Urge to Merge

Large corporations sometimes have the capability of raising large amounts of capital. At times, they might decide to buy a competitor to gain a greater share of a particular market. They could buy a business that is in trouble, hoping that they are getting a bargain and can turn it around. They also can buy a company that has nothing to do with what they produce. Regardless, whenever one company absorbs another it is called a **merger.** Depending upon the situation, the bought company may lose its identity altogether.

There are three types of mergers that take place in American business:

- **Horizontal Merger**—a merger of two companies that offer the same good or service; for example, if Ameritech and Bell Atlantic merged, it would be a horizontal merger.
- **Vertical Merger**—a merger of two companies at different phases of the production of the same good or service; for example, when Andrew Carnegie's steel company bought a coal mine and railroad, he wanted to control every phase of the production of his steel.
- **Conglomerates**—a merger of two or more companies that offer different goods or services; for example, if GM were to buy a hotel chain and a phone company, it would be building a conglomerate.

Depending upon the economist you talk to, a merger can be both a positive and negative occurrence. Merged companies can improve their decision-making process, combine capital resources, and expand production potential by using already existing factories. Mergers are especially appreciated by the stockholders of the acquired company. The value of their stock usually climbs when another company buys them out. On the other hand, the value of the stock in the purchasing company will often decrease. Furthermore, a newly merged company may lack the decision-making ability to handle its new size. Critics also argue that consumers will have to pay higher prices for products due to the reduction in competition in the case of horizontal mergers.

The Pressing Question

12. Which is more important—private property and business autonomy or consumer protection and freedom of choice? Why do you think so?

I. Oligopolies

Market structure will never reach a perfect monopoly or perfect competition. It is important for us to understand them both, because it becomes easier to spot the imperfections in our own economy. One prominent type of imperfect competition is called **oligopoly**. It exists when the largest three or four companies dominate more than approximately 70 percent of the industry's total output. The auto industry in the United States is a good example of an oligopoly.

In certain market situations, such as automobiles and airlines, there is not much choice involved. The Department of Justice and Federal Trade Commission watch closely for price violations.

In the 1920s, there were many car companies in the United States. However, some corporations have merged, gone out of business, or left the market for one reason or another. In some markets, consumers do not have too many choices between producers offering similar products. On the other hand, global producers have moved into the American market. One can buy a Volvo (Swedish), and Audi (German), or a Toyota (Japanese). The 1990s also saw mergers between foreign and American auto companies. Thus, the auto market remains quite competitive dispute the small number of auto producers.

Price is not always determined by the consumer in an oligopoly. If the largest company wishes to raise market price, it will raise the price of a chosen product. It hopes that the smaller companies will follow suit. If they do, a new price is set. If they do not, the large company will be forced to bring its price back down.

While **price leadership** is considered acceptable by U.S. antitrust law, other methods of determining price are not. If companies conspire with one another to set prices or production levels, it is known as **collusion**. Because the consumers are not part of the determination of price or production, collusion is strictly prohibited by law.

The Pressing Questions

13. List the four criteria for the existence of an oligopoly.

14. How might a few big companies violate antitrust law?

J. The History of Labor in the United States

Most people have a strong opinion about unions in our country today. For some, loyalty to unions knows no boundaries. They will never cross a picket line and tend to look for products that were made by other union workers. On the other hand, some people distrust unions and believe that the labor market should be left alone. They think that businesses are stifled by the high costs of union labor and the attempts of unions to control the production process. Whatever the opinion, there was a time when the purpose of unions was most clearly defined.

From the very beginning of our country, labor organizations of some sort have been present. They took their structure from medieval guilds of Europe. Their function was to set prices, assign product guidelines, and train new workers. A young apprentice would join a guild family and begin learning the trade. After years of service, around the age of 16, the apprentice would become a journeyman, and was then allowed to offer his services to other employers. Finally, when the young man had created his greatest work, his masterpiece, he was then made a master in the guild.

Therefore, the earliest guilds and unions in the United States were exclusive to those people who had a specific skill. For example, shoemakers, cigar rollers, and printers each had a union in the United States by the 1790s. But, because these all were skills that took years to acquire, members of **craft unions** set themselves apart from common laborers.

As America became more industrialized through the mid-1800s, more craft unions began to form. They had a lot to defend. The life of a skilled craftsman was much more desirable than that of an unskilled laborer. Picture a shoemaker who, with five other workers, makes the shoes for an entire town. The sewing, cutting, and stitching were all complicated tasks that took years to learn. His product was of the highest quality. Life in the store was relatively relaxed, and the camaraderie of the workers made the work much easier.

But, when the shoe factory opened up outside of town, its shoes sold at a fraction of the cost of the shoemaker's shoes. The factory did mean lower prices and higher quantities of shoes. But because of the lack of business, the skilled workers had to close up shop and look for work in the factory. At that point, the jobs they once had of making an entire shoe were broken down into the simplest of tasks—so simple that anyone could be hired to do it. Because of the lack of skill needed to make the shoes in mass production, the workers could not demand high wages. If one complained, he or she was simply dismissed and replaced. The first need for **labor unions**, or unions for unskilled workers, became evident.

Workers in factories had to contend with many problems. First of all, they had to work twelve- to fourteen-hour days for very low wages. The working conditions were often unsafe, noisy, and unsanitary. Few benefits were offered. If workers got sick or injured on the job, they were replaced by other willing workers. Unskilled workers brought nothing to the table but their labor. When they stood up for their rights by themselves, they had no power over what the company might do. However, if they all stood up together, they might be heard.

A variety of craft unions and federations of craft unions existed in the 1800s, but the first union in U.S. history to cater to unskilled workers was known as the **Knights of Labor**. Started as a secret organization in the late 1860s, the Knights sought to accept all workers—no matter what their skill level, gender, or race. By 1886, the Knights had close to 700,000 members. It advocated the replacement of capitalism with a system of worker cooperatives. Because of this and other radical ideas, the Knights slowly faded from prominence by the 1890s. It lingered until it dissolved in 1917.

Of the many issues sought by unions of the time, none were voiced more vociferously than by the **American Federation of Labor** (AFL). Founded in 1886 by Samuel Gompers, the AFL was a federation of smaller craft unions. Gompers and his followers were most noted for their support of "bread and butter unionism." This meant that they pursued the basic issues like an eight-hour workday, no child labor, safer working conditions, and higher wages. The AFL expanded throughout the first half of the twentieth century. As will be discussed later, it still exists in some form today.

Early unions like the Knights and the AFL had a limited amount of options when it came to getting what they wanted. First, they could **strike**, or refuse to go into work. This would be accompanied by a **picket line**. Workers marched outside their place of employment and tried to draw public attention to their cause. Hopefully, they could start a **boycott** of the company's products to influence a speedy response from management. If matters escalated, a **secondary boycott**, or a refusal to buy any products that are associated with the company in question, could be enacted. Other times, workers could fight back with less formal tactics like the **slowdown,** where the pace of production would gradually stall. But, in the end, the hope was to sit down with the owners of the company to negotiate a settlement. This was the ultimate goal—**collective bargaining**.

Rarely did the bosses take this lying down. Most industrialists hated the idea of unions. They believed in an idea called **Social Darwinism**. They thought that people who succeeded in life were genetically superior to others. In other words, some people were born with the talent to rise to the top, and some were born to be poor. This ideal only strengthened their resolve against the budding unions. To combat them, companies used an assortment of tactics:

- **Scab labor**—Companies would hire replacement workers.
- **Yellow dog contracts**—Companies would hire only people who would sign a contract promising they would not strike.
- **Pinkertons**—These were hired agents that would infiltrate the unions or simply use violence to break up picket lines.
- **Blacklists**—The company would compile a list of union members and distribute it to all the other companies. If you were on the list, you could not get a job.
- **Injunctions**—The company would ask (or sometimes bribe) local officials, especially judges, to order the workers back into the factory. If workers refused, they were arrested.
- **Runaway shops**—If union activity grew too intense in an area, bosses would merely move to another area of the country where the workforce was less organized.
- **Scientific management**—Developed by thinkers like Frederick Taylor, this practice broke down every task, even shoveling coal, into the tiniest motion. Workers had to follow the rules implicitly.

- **Business organizations**—Owners exchanged ideas about keeping workers happy or breaking strikes more effectively through vehicles like the Chambers of Commerce, which appeared throughout the country around the turn of the twentieth century.

Needless to say, unions grew irritated at these tactics and often would lash out against the companies. These violent outbreaks—like Chicago's Haymarket Affair where eight policemen died when a bomb was tossed into a crowd—brought a bad name to the unions. They were labeled as radical, socialist, and violent. Unfortunately, many unions fit these descriptions.

John L. Lewis, the president of the United Mine Workers of America, defied the AFL leadership and formed the **Congress of Industrial Organizations** (CIO), the first successful union for unskilled workers. Started in the 1930s, the CIO opened its ranks to women and minorities. Because of this, it stood in opposition to the AFL for many years. In 1955, the two unions joined to form the AFL-CIO, which is today the single biggest labor organization in the United States.

Union membership hit a peak during World War II. Bad publicity and corruption, a shift to white-collar jobs, and lack of government support have all led to a decline in union membership. Today, less than 14 percent of the workforce belongs to a union. In the 1980s, the federal government sided with businesses in several high-profile strikes. In the 1990s, unions found themselves having to shift with the times. Despite this, organized labor remains a formidable political force in the United States.

In 1935, unions like the CIO got a boost from the federal government with the National Labor Relations Act. This gave unions for the first time the right to bargain collectively. It also formed the National Labor Relations Board to **mediate** disputes. If the problem is serious, the board might choose to **arbitrate** the problem by suggesting solutions. If that does not help, the board will use **binding arbitration**. This means that the suggested solutions must be followed.

Historically, unions never fared well in times of economic distress. Depressions of the 1800s, like those in 1873 and 1893, sent members scrambling for any job they could get. Strikes were usually in vain, because

The Minimum Wage since 1950

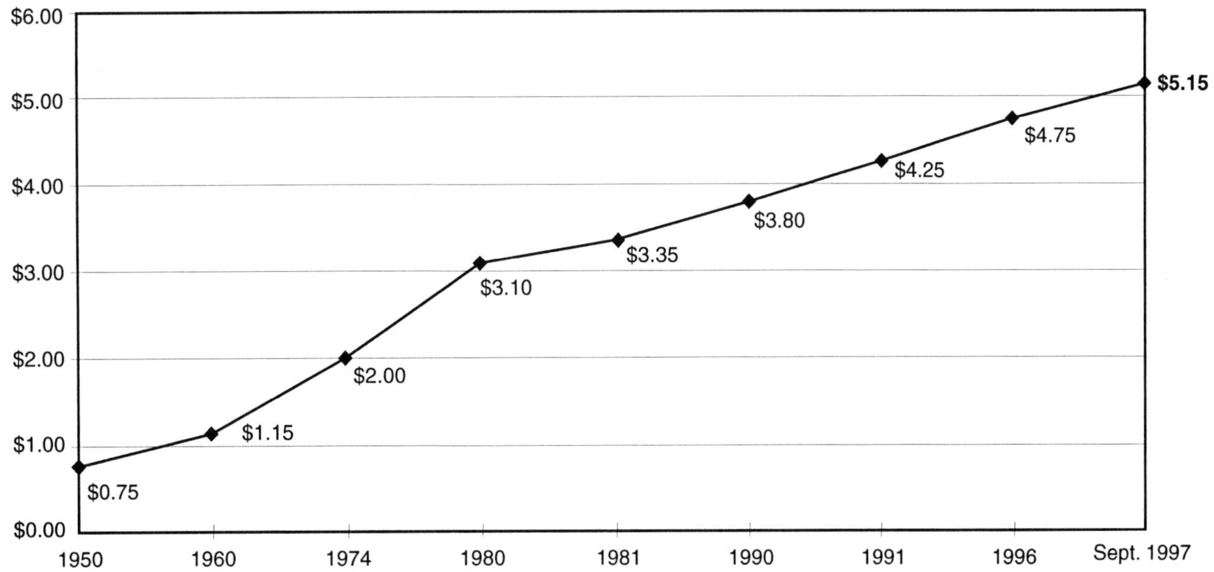

Source: U.S. Department of Labor

replacement labor was so plentiful. Ironically, the worst economy of the twentieth century brought unions their greatest hour. This happened for several reasons.

Unions succeeded in the 1930s because many of the unemployed refused to cross picket lines. Councils formed by unions made sure that people got fed during many strikes. Second, unions were more organized. Led by John L. Lewis, the CIO actually planned strikes strategically industry by industry instead of waiting for them to happen. Third, governments were pro-labor for the first time in U.S. history. Governors refused to use the national guard against strikers, and judges refused injunctions. In the end, all the law did was try to keep the peace, and the business owners were on their own.

The Pressing Question

15. Considering the past issues fought for by unions, what do you believe are the four most important issues or needs of all American workers today?

K. Our Changing Labor Force

The **labor force** is defined as all of the people over the age of sixteen in the country who are working or looking for work. Not included in this number are people who cannot work for some physical or mental reason. There are also people who have stopped looking for employment. Those under sixteen who have a job are included, although those under sixteen without work are not. It is important to remember the exact definition of labor force, because it will help clarify exactly what unemployment means.

In the past 150 years, there has been a radical shift in what Americans do for a living. The percentage of farm workers dropped from 90 percent in 1800 to about 63 percent in 1850. By 1900, only 38 percent of the workers were agricultural. Today, we can find only 3 percent of our workforce on farms. Furthermore, in the last twenty years, there has been a radical drop in the number of manufacturing jobs. Most workers in America are employed in service industries. In other words, they aren't building cars and machines; they are health care workers, accountants, computer programmers, engineers, restaurant workers, etc.

While many service sector jobs (like those in high-tech fields) require advanced training, many offer wages much lower than work in manufacturing. A good education is essential to job security.

People today worry about the security of their jobs. It is not uncommon for someone to switch jobs or careers six to ten times in a lifetime. The only way to ensure that you have control of your occupation is to make sure you develop a skill that is in high demand. At the turn of this century, it is clear that computers are the essential tools of our society. People who are skilled in programming, maintaining, and developing computers are eagerly sought by employers. In any event, lifelong learning is critical. The ability and willingness to constantly learn new job-related skills is essential.

The Pressing Question

16. Considering all of the trends in the labor force mentioned in the reading, do you believe that the United States is headed in the right direction or the wrong direction? Explain your belief.

L. Wage Issues

People's **wages** are the amount of money they receive in exchange for their labor. Most people are either paid by the hour or paid a flat yearly **salary**. However they are paid, there are a number of factors that can contribute to how much money a person makes.

First, just as they do in determining the price of a product, supply and demand dictate the value of a person's labor. If the occupation requires the worker to have very specific skills, the small number of qualified candidates will push the cost of labor higher. Also, if the location of the job is isolated, there will be few people available. Third, when jobs are highly dangerous, few people will be willing to do the work. In any of these situations, labor will be very expensive. Remember, if the supply is low or the demand is high, wages will move upward.

The government also tries to maintain control over the wages that people get. Since 1938, in the **Fair Labor Standards Act**, there has been a minimum wage in the United States. Starting at $.25/hour in 1938, the smallest legal amount an employer is allowed to pay for most occupations is $5.15. (Waiters and waitresses can be paid less because of tip income.)

Lastly, unions have an impact on wages. One of the main demands of unions today is higher wages. When a factory brings in union labor, the cost of labor will limit the amount of workers that can be hired. While the people employed will be making more, there will not be as many jobs.

In the end, it is essential that workers today attain and maintain a skill that is in demand if they want to maintain their standards of living. Lifelong learning is essential.

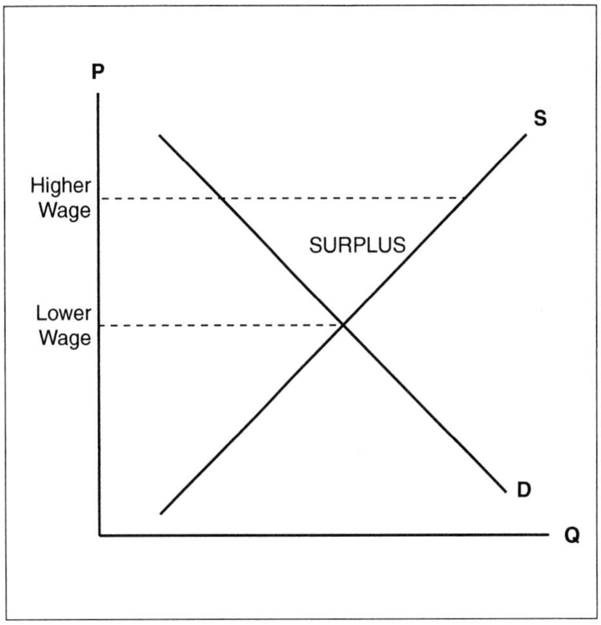

Few people realize that artificially imposed higher wages may have an adverse impact on the labor market. A rise in the minimum wage may actually cause more people to be out of work.

The Pressing Question

17. Figure out what a full-time minimum wage worker makes in a year.

Name________________________

Date________________________

Business Basics

Directions: With the help of your reading or from outside sources like a dictionary or encyclopedia, provide a definition for each of the following terms. Be prepared to discuss your definition.

1. venture capital

2. sole proprietorship

3. liability

4. partnership

5. private corporation

6. public corporation

7. capital gains tax

8. dividend

9. initial public offering

10. nonprofit corporation

Name_______________________

Date_______________________

11. internal financing

12. law of diminishing returns

13. production possibilities

14. fixed costs

15. variable costs

16. marginal costs

17. monopoly

18. oligopoly

19. perfect competition

20. Justice Department

Name____________________________

Date____________________________

21. Sherman Antitrust Act

22. trust

23. merger

24. Federal Trade Commission

25. conglomerate

26. arbitration

27. mediator

28. labor force

29. salary

30. Fair Standards Act

Name____________________________

Date____________________________

Business Organizations

Part A.

Directions: Using your reading as a guide, fill in the following chart with details about each business formation.

Type of Business	Definition	Example	Advantage	Disadvantage
sole proprietorship				
partnership				
nonprofit				
cooperative				
corporation				

Name________________________

Date________________________

Part B.

Directions: Answer the following questions.

1. What are some different ways to make money from investing in a company?

2. What are some of the various ways a corporation can combine?

3. What makes a franchise an appealing investment to many people?

4. What role do nonprofits play in our economy? How does the government encourage their survival?

5. What is the difference between a public and a private corporation? Give examples of each.

6. List three examples for each of the following: sole proprietorships you deal with, corporations you deal with, nonprofits you deal with.

7. What are some of the different ways that businesses can access capital for expansion?

Name______________________

Date______________________

Beginning in Business

Directions: In your small group, decide upon a business you would like to start. Then write a business plan specific to the goal of the venture. List on the chart the items that you think you would need to start serving customers.

Business Plan

Items Needed to Start the Business	Estimated Cost

Total Cost for Start-Up ______________

Name______________________________

Date______________________________

Business Flow Chart

Directions: For each of the following steps, fill in the chart with the appropriate terms. If you have trouble, refer to your reading.

Irene did the following:	This is actually called a
1. formed a small business in which she is the only owner and assumed full liability	______________________
2. found someone to share the risk with and take some of the responsibility	______________________
3. wrote down the purpose and focus of her business	______________________
4. borrowed money in the form of a business loan from a financial institution	______________________
5. incorporated her small business with her state of origin	______________________
6. wrote legally binding agreements with her suppliers and customers	______________________
7. paid workers set amounts every two weeks	______________________
8. sought additional capital from investors by selling stock in her company to the public	______________________
9. kept some of her profits in the company to allow for faster growth	______________________
10. sold the licensing rights to sell her products in stores that will look just like hers	______________________
11. split the profits among all the stockholders, thereby giving them their fair share	______________________
12. was named the head of the company	______________________
13. divided her company into smaller pieces for sale to the public	______________________
14. borrowed money straight from investors for a set amount of time at a set interest rate	______________________

Word Bank

business charter	dividends	partner
bank	internal financing	contracts
bond	sole proprietorship	business plan
chief executive officer	initial public offering	salary
franchise	stock	

Name________________________

Date________________________

Monopolies

Part A.

Directions: Complete the following chart, using your reading as a guide.

Business Formation	Number of Companies Competing	Entry to Market	Information	Control of Prices	Choice for Consumers
Perfect competition					
Oligopoly					
Monopoly					

Part B.

Directions: Answer the following questions.

1. What is the traditional gift given to a woman at the time of engagement?

2. Why are diamonds considered to be so precious?

3. Where did the tradition come from?

Name____________________________

Date_____________________________

4. How much is the man supposed to pay for the gift?

5. What company controls most of the world's diamond supply?

6. Draw a supply and demand graph that you think accurately represents the market for diamonds.

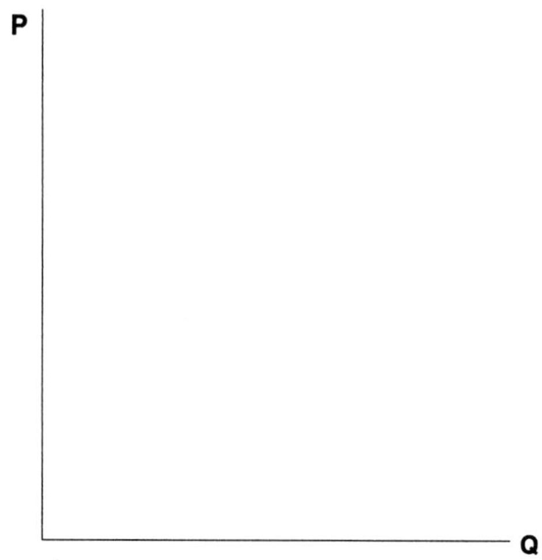

7. How does this hurt the American consumer?

Name________________________

Date________________________

The Sherman Antitrust Act

Directions: After carefully reading the excerpt from the act itself, answer the questions. If you need help, refer to **Handout 8**.

SEC. 1. Every contract, combination in the form of trust or otherwise, or conspiracy, in restraint of trade or commerce among the several States, or with foreign nations, is hereby declared to be illegal. Every person who shall make any such contract or engage in any such combination or conspiracy, shall be deemed guilty of a misdemeanor, and, on conviction thereof, shall be punished by fine not exceeding five thousand dollars, or by imprisonment not exceeding one year, or by both said punishments, in the discretion of the court.

SEC. 2. Every person who shall monopolize, or attempt to monopolize, or combine or conspire with any other person or persons, to monopolize any part of the trade or commerce among the several States, or with foreign nations, shall be deemed guilty of a misdemeanor, and, on conviction thereof, shall be punished by fine not exceeding five thousand dollars, or by imprisonment not exceeding one year, or by both said punishments, in the discretion of the court.

SEC. 3. Every contract, combination in form of trust or otherwise, or conspiracy, in restraint of trade or commerce in any Territory of the United States or of the District of Columbia, or . . . with foreign nations, . . . is hereby declared illegal. . . .

SEC. 4. The several circuit courts of the United States are hereby invested with jurisdiction to prevent and restrain violations of this act; and it shall be the duty of the several district attorneys of the United States, in their respective districts, under the direction of the Attorney General, to institute proceedings in equity to prevent and restrain such violations. . . . When the parties complained of shall have been duly notified of such petition the court shall proceed, as soon as may be, to the hearing and determination of the case; and . . . the court may at any time make such temporary restraining order or prohibition as shall be deemed just in the premises. . . .

SEC. 7. Any person who shall be injured in his business or property by any other person or corporation by reason of anything forbidden or declared to be unlawful by this act, may sue . . . without respect to the amount in controversy, and shall recover threefold the damages by him sustained, and the costs of suit, including a reasonable attorney's fee.

SEC. 8. That the word "person," or "persons," wherever used in this act shall be deemed to include corporations and associations existing under or authorized by the laws of either the United States, the laws of any of the Territories, the laws of any State, or the laws of any foreign country.

1. Who wrote this law?

2. When was it written?

Name________________________

Date________________________

3. What three-word phrase in Section 1 describes what exactly is illegal?

4. What sorts of businesses, about one hundred years ago, were first prosecuted under this law?

5. Who is in charge of enforcing this law?

6. What was the initial penalty for violating this law?

7. What is a fair punishment now?

8. What company was split apart due to violation of this law in 1983?

9. What computer software company had to defend its conduct in the late 1990s when it was accused of violating the Sherman Act?

10. Who makes the decisions about a company's behavior according to this law?

Name________________________

Date________________________

Labor Research Assignment

Directions: Research one of the following topics and complete the items below. You will have to present your information in class, so make your research thorough but concise.

1. John L. Lewis
2. Bill Haywood
3. Samuel Gompers
4. Jimmy Hoffa
5. Terrence Powderly
6. Molly Maguires
7. Pinkertons
8. Haymarket Massacre
9. 1937 Flint Sit-Down Strike
10. 1981 Air-Traffic Controllers' Strike

Name: ________________________________ Years: ________________________________

a. Organizations involved with (or in)

b. The significance of this individual or event

c. Other famous people involved with this person or event

d. A brief biography of this person or origins of this event

e. A brief (approximately thirty words) summary of this event or individual

Name____________________

Date____________________

Supply and Demand for Labor

Directions: For each scenario, complete the following steps.

- Decide whether the supply of labor or the demand for labor will change.
- Label the graph given.
- Draw and label the new supply or demand curve.
- Indicate what happened to wages for those workers.

Example:

The computer industry is suddenly in need of workers who have high-tech training.

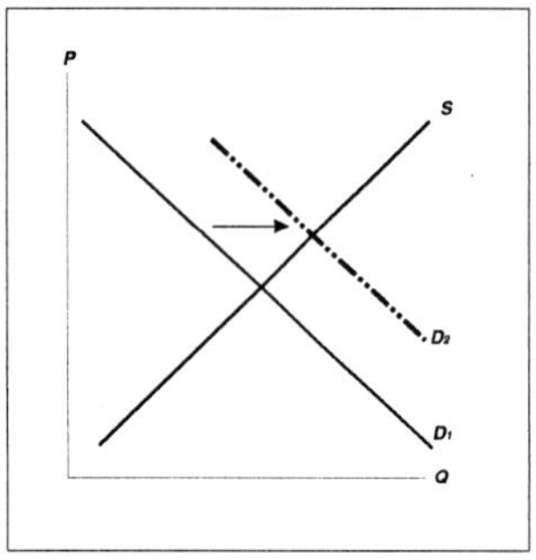

Change in labor?

The demand for labor will increase.

Change in wages?

Wages will increase.

1. The economy is very hot. Overall, jobs are being created and not filled.

Change in labor?

____

Change in wages?

____

2. You work on an assembly line, and companies across the country are buying robots to do your job.

Change in labor?

____

Change in wages?

____

Name_______________________

Date_______________________

3. The number of sheet metal workers has declined due to the lack of high school graduates entering the trade.

Change in labor?

____

Change in wages?

____

4. Congress just raised minimum wage from \$5.15 an hour to \$8.00 an hour. What would that price floor look like?

Change in labor?

____

Change in wages?

____

5. In the next twenty years, half of all teachers will be retiring.

Change in labor?

____

Change in wages?

____

Part 3
Financial Institutions

Questions to Consider

1. What is money?
2. How does money make life easier?
3. How do banks make money?
4. How do banks fail?
5. Why is productivity so vital to our nation's health?
6. How do we slip into recessions?
7. Why do prices go up?
8. How is inflation bad?
9. Why have a national bank?
10. Who should be in charge of it?
11. What power does the Federal Reserve need to function?
12. Is it effective?

Terms You Need in Order to Read

Inflation	Economy	Monetary policy
Recession	Productivity	Interest

Name________________________

Date________________________

Financial Institutions

Directions: Read the selection, and answer the Pressing Questions as you read. Be prepared for class discussion.

A. The History of Money

Think back to our earlier discussions about economics. In part 1, you learned that an economy exists whenever people produce things and consume things (or provide and require services). The constant transfer of goods that goes along with vibrant economy needs help to succeed. Even in smaller countries, an economy would shut down without a viable medium of exchange. In other words, any financial transaction where goods or services are exchanged needs something to come between the producer and the consumer.

If we did not have money, we would be forced to barter, or exchange goods without the help of money. Let's say you grew some corn. You also need a new pair of tennis shoes. You set out across town with a car full of corn only to discover that many people would love to have your corn, but none of these people have any shoes that you would like. In essence, you have to find someone who has what you want and wants what you have. This is called the **double coincidence of wants**.

In the earliest economies that developed all over the world, people must have quickly lost patience. They quickly figured out that there were certain things that everyone wanted. People began to accumulate these goods. These things are called **commodities**. Depending on the area of the world, they could be seashells, animals, precious metals, or an agricultural product. We call this commodity **money**.

All over the world, certain substances seemed to be universally desired. Some substances—like gold—were more desired than others. They have an intrinsic value. The next logical step was to take those precious metals and press them, or mint them, into coins. The Chinese were the first to do this during the Chou dynasty almost 3,000 years ago. In the western world, Lydians, who lived on the Mediterranean, issued their own coins to aid in a bustling commerce at about 1200 B.C. From that point forward, civilized people like the Greeks, Romans, and Muslims used precious coins made of gold and silver to make commerce easier—and more profitable!

In the Renaissance, bankers noticed that coins made of precious metals would constantly be tampered with as consumers would shave off some of the coin and then pass it off as whole. A vendor would accept it not noticing the difference. The next consumers and vendors may also tamper with it. The result in the end would be a mangled piece of currency that held little of its original value. In essence, when an economy tries to use **specie** (gold or silver coins) as its **currency**, bad money will always drive out the good money. We call this **Gresham's Law**.

Governments wanted to make sure they could make every little bit of tax that they could from their countries' lively trade, so they came up with a solution. Keep the precious metals in a safe somewhere, and issue bills that represented the gold or silver. This is called **representative money**. In the 1700s, countries all over the world began to issue their own commodity-backed currency . . . except the United States.

Aside from its aesthetics, most industrialized countries keep reserves of gold. In the last few decades however, gold has steadily lost value and its appeal as a basis for currency value.

Instead of having our own national currency, our founding fathers left money to be an issue of the states. Bank notes were issued by independent banks, and consumers and travelers were left to figure it out for themselves. Worst of all, if a bank failed, you would be left with worthless paper. It was not until the Civil War that the United States had its own national currency. (The Confederates had their own as well.) The currency was black on the front, but the bright green ink used to print the backs gave them the nickname we still use for our money today—greenbacks.

Do you recognize these representative currencies?

This representative currency served us well until 1971 when Congress passed the Gold Reserve Act. Our currency was no longer backed by gold! It merely has value because the government says it does. The Latin word for a government decree is *fiat*. Therefore, we call the currency in the United States **fiat currency**.

The Pressing Question

1. After reading the preceding passage, try to come up with a good definition for the word **money**. Write your definition below.

B. Guide to Useful Money

Think about the last time you spent a significant amount of money. Let's say you bought a few CDs and then went to lunch with some friends. Different items that you purchased were given a value according to our currency. Items of higher value required more money to obtain. Our dollar helps us set the **standard of value** for various goods and services.

To be useful, money must first be an accepted **medium of exchange**. In other words, when people exchange goods, money will come between them to define a value of the good or service. Next, it must hold its value over time. You may have heard stories of people hiding their money in a mattress or in a vase in a backyard garden. A good currency will keep its value over a long period of time. This is called a **store of value.**

Money must have some other properties in order to be useful to an economy. Because transactions rarely equal an exact dollar, our currency must be easily divided into a fraction. Furthermore, it must be widely recognized by people so that there is widespread faith that the money is **legal tender**. This means that it may be used to settle any debts—public or private.

Lastly, a good money has to last. The Department of the Treasury has long tried to find a dollar bill that can take the punishment that we tend to give it. Despite all of their efforts, the average dollar bill lasts only about a year and a half. There has been some discussion of phasing out the dollar bill and replacing it with a coin. The main reason for this is the added durability the U.S. Mint could offer in a new coin. The Susan B. Anthony dollar coin was not a success. It is too early to judge the success of the Sacajawea dollar coin.

The Pressing Question

2. In order for our modern money to be useful. It must have certain attributes. Each of the important attributes is listed below. Define them.

   a. Portability

   b. Durability

   c. Divisibility

   d. Store of Value

   e. Standard of Value

C. The Money Supply

To have any sort of value, the supply of money has to be finite. Like anything, scarcity will give it a certain value. If there is more money printed, it will lose value. If money is taken out of circulation, it will gain value. This fact can affect prices of all of the products in our economy. Because of this, economists watch the money supply very closely. In total, our money supply exceeds six trillion dollars. That sounds like a lot of money, but its scarcity demands that we compete for it.

Think about the adults in your life. Do you think that most of their money is kept in currency somewhere in the house or in their wallets? Chances are, like most Americans, the bulk of their money is kept in a checking account. The money held in these accounts is considered so liquid that economists consider that it might as well be cash. With bills, mortgages, and tuition payments, most paychecks never even get changed into cash. They are merely deposited and transferred from one bank to another. As you can see, most money in our economy isn't even in the form of dollars and coins. Most of it is almost cash, what we call **demand deposits** (most commonly in checking accounts). In other words, deposits are "payable on demand."

The money supply can be broken down as follows:

- **M1**—Economists argue about this category all the time. This is currency, traveler's checks, and different types of checking accounts.
- **M2**—This includes any money that is kept in any short-term investment that allows a person quick access to his or her money. These are called **near monies**. Chief among these are money market and savings accounts. Banks invest in different bonds and securities in bulk and pass the interest benefits on to the investor.
- **M3**—This includes types of bonds.

To get a good idea of what our money supply looks like, refer to the graph that illustrates the components of M2.

Components of M2, 1999

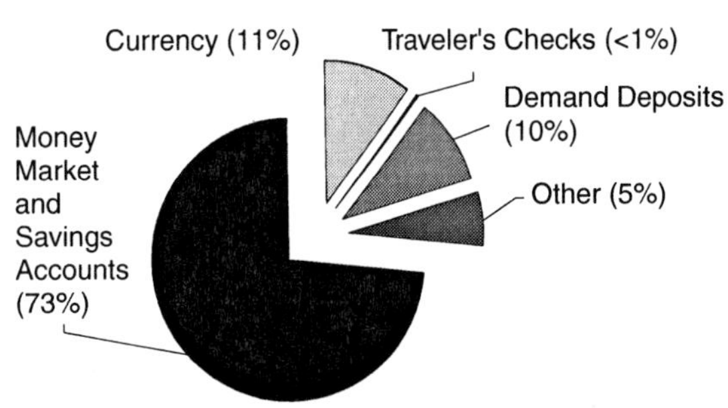

Source: Department of the Treasury

The Pressing Question

3. What do you suppose happens to prices across the economy if the money supply increases?

D. Our Dollar Overseas

Although the number is difficult to gauge, some economists estimate that almost 75 percent of U.S. currency is held by people overseas. In fact, dollars are the more trusted in emerging markets like Russia because of the instability of their own governments. Unfortunately, there is a cost that goes along with this newfound popularity.

Counterfeiting has become a favorite activity of organized crime and governments across the world. One particular bill, called the "superbill," is so convincing that many banks are fooled. This has meant that the one hundred dollar bill is often refused by merchants and financial houses overseas. This issue has been vigorously pursued by the **Secret Service,** which has recommended to the U.S. Treasury Department that they create new security measures to discourage would-be counterfeit operations.

For the most part, our money is secure. This is a great comfort to those of us who choose to travel overseas. More importantly, what about the thousands of American companies that do business in other countries. If they sell something in another country, they will eventually have to convert that currency to U.S. dollars. They do this with deposit money or electronic wire transfers. This is only possible with the help of foreign **exchange markets.**

There are markets all over the world in which people do nothing but buy and sell money all day. For instance, if a trader holds one million U.S. dollars and converts it to five million French francs, he or she will hope that the franc will **strengthen** (or gain value) against the dollar. Thus, after an hour, week, or month, the trader can change the money back to dollars. More U.S. money will be required to equal the five million francs. In the end, the whole venture could potentially net (or lose) tens of thousands of dollars.

What happens if you are a business that does business in France? You hope that the French will buy more of your product. Supposing that the price in France remained constant, higher sales should mean higher profits for your company. But if the dollar **weakens** (or loses value), it will take less francs to equal the dollars in your retail price. When the francs are changed into dollars, you will get more dollars for each franc that is exchanged. The result is higher sales and profits for your American business.

The U.S. government, realizing this trend, watched the value of the dollar in the eighties. A weaker dollar actually reduced the prices of certain products overseas. Our products became more competitive.

The currency markets around the world fluctuate in value according to **floating exchange rates**. Japan has suggested that the nations of the world convert to a **fixed exchange rate** as was used between 1944 and 1973. Back then, the United States forced the change because foreign countries were constantly redeeming their dollars for gold which helped to deplete our national gold reserves.

The Pressing Questions

4. Is it better for the U.S. dollar to be stronger or weaker?

5. If you are an international traveler, do you want a stronger or a weaker dollar? Why?

E. How Banks Create Money

When you think about banks, the first thing that probably comes to mind is the safe. The primary function of banks is to be a depository for people's money. But how do banks make money? As long as we are talking about money, it is about time we discussed the concept of interest.

If you have ever borrowed money from someone, you may have given them an IOU with a promise to pay them at a later date. In the world of business, it is pretty much the same thing. When you borrow money from someone, they will want something in return. They will charge you a percentage of the **principal** that you borrowed per year. This is called the annual percentage rate (**APR**). For instance, if you borrow $100,000 at 10 percent interest, you will owe the servicer of the loan $10,000 at the end of the first year. That comes to almost $840 per month to pay off the interest alone. Now you know why people who have a mortgage complain as much as they do.

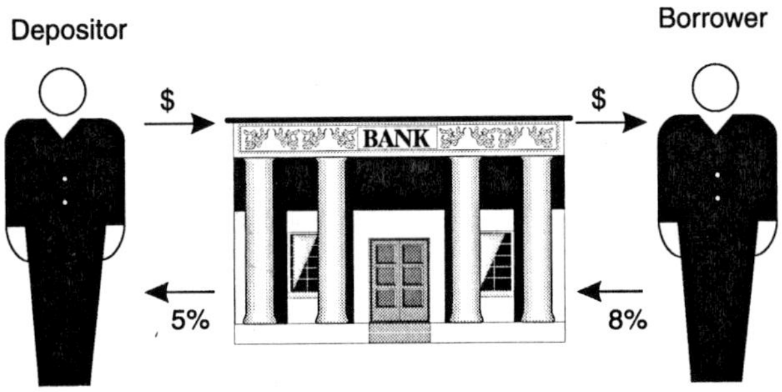

Banks take loaning money very seriously. They must follow many government regulations that help discern between good risks and bad risks. The government has been involved in the process since the 1930s when Congress established the Federal Deposit Insurance Corporation (**FDIC**). After the Great Depression forced many banks to close, many Americans who saw their life savings lost refused to trust banks again. To remedy this, the FDIC guaranteed all deposits up to a certain amount. Today, the amount insured is $100,000. Next time you hear a commercial for a bank, listen closely for the "FDIC insured" at the end.

The Pressing Questions

6. How does a bank fail (go out of business)?

7. If a bank is making 10 percent on money it loans out, how much interest do you think it pays depositors?

8. Bank failures in the past are referred to as "runs." How did they get that name?

F. Banking Today

A person who needs to borrow or save has several options in today's marketplace. Some of the institutions you have to choose from are as follows:

- **Commercial Banks** are the most numerous, profitable, and stable. National City, Key Bank, and Citibank are counted among this category.

- **Credit Unions** are commonly associated with unions, churches, and other fraternal organizations. Members deposit their money in order to buy shares that pay an annual interest. Because they sometimes use volunteer labor and capital contributed by a sponsor organization, a credit union is able to loan out money to members at lower rates than commercial banks. Also, credit unions are not taxed on their income while other depository institutions are.

Each depository institution offers different advantages and disadvantages. The wise consumer shops for a financial institution as one would for a car or even a loaf of bread.

While you are very used to ATMs, they are relatively new to banking. As with most technology, they make life easier while complicating it at the same time. Why is that?

One last development in banking today is the rapid proliferation of automatic teller machines. These make things like demand deposits even more liquid. Debit cards can be used like credit cards while they take money directly from one's checking account. The wise consumer always keeps receipts and keeps close track of his or her spending. In the past, a check could take 5 to 7 days of **float time** to clear. Currently, debits happen almost instantaneously.

The Pressing Questions

9. Now that you know what a credit union is, form a definition for the word *credit*. Write it below.

10. Which loan is the most expensive (in interest rates) to get—a car loan or a long-term home mortgage? Why?

11. What does it mean to bounce a check?

G. Productivity in the United States

One of the most important jobs of our government is to keep a close eye on our economy. If you have ever heard someone say, "I think the economy is doing terribly," did you ever wonder what that person was talking about? Taking into consideration that an economy exists whenever people get together to make and consume goods and services, the United States makes an extraordinary amount of goods every year. If we take the dollar value of every single product that is made and add it together, the final calculation is known as the **gross domestic product**. In 1996, that number reached almost eight trillion dollars.

The whole point to starting a business is to maximize your profits. Let's say you own a putter factory. Your employees are able to manufacture 2,000 putters a month at their maximum efficiency. Your putters are selling well, so you declare to the staff that you wish the factory to hit a goal of 2,200 putters next month. Is it possible? Can you do it without hiring more workers? The answer may be "yes."

You need your people to become more **productive.** This would mean the benefits to your firm by making more goods would exceed the value of the costs. Your company should try to figure out new ways of becoming more efficient. Time has to be used more effectively. Machines need to be geared to operate more quickly. If all goes well, your goals could possibly be met. Sales will meet the high demand, and your profits will rise. The best thing is, you didn't have to spend any more money to produce more. However, this is rarely possible since most technology is embodied in new capital goods.

As a country, we also want to become more productive. In essence, the United States needs to produce more goods this year than it did last year. If we do, there will be more jobs for our citizens, more profits for our companies, and more prosperity all around. The gross domestic product (GDP) is perhaps the most important piece of information calculated by the government. It is vital that our country's companies and citizens continue to become more productive in their work. Because adding together all of these numbers is difficult, GDP is calculated by using a formula. By adding together these four things, a dollar value that equals our GDP can be reached:

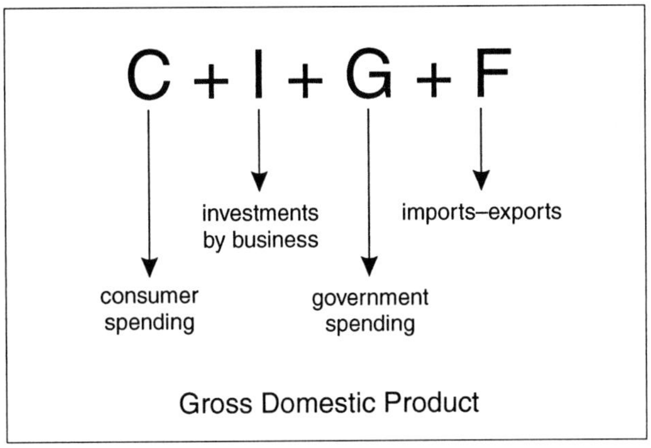

Of the four categories in GDP, our consumer spending is by far the largest. Around 65 percent of our eight-trillion-dollar yearly consumption comes from the consumer sector. That is why the United States is considered the most fertile market on earth and often referred to as a "consumer society."

GDP can also help us figure out how much each citizen in our country produces. We divide our population by our current GDP to get **per capita GDP**. Lastly, because the value of a dollar changes every year, we compensate for inflation by figuring out our **real (or per capita) GDP**.

The Pressing Question

12. Give three examples of goods or services that fit into each of the following categories:
    a. consumer spending

    b. investment spending

    c. governmental spending

H. Recessions: An Economy's Second-Worst Nightmare

If a good economy depends on a lot of production and consumption, a bad economy lacks in one of the two. Sometimes, for a variety of reasons, people stop buying things. When they do, factories will have to slow production. If that happens, layoffs are sure to follow. With people out of work, they will usually not be in the mood to go out and buy any big-ticket items like cars or appliances. This, in turn, will cause the factories to slow down even more. When business activity stalls to a visible extent, we call that a **recession**.

When a recession takes place, one of the symptoms is higher unemployment rates. **Unemployment** is defined as the situation when people do not have a job but are actively seeking another. The rate itself is computed by dividing the number of people who are unemployed by the number of people in the labor force. The labor force does not include people under sixteen, those who cannot work, and those who have stopped looking for work. In the American population of 270 million people, approximately 120 million people are considered part of the labor force. Unemployment should never hit 0 percent, though. At the best of times, when the economy is strongest, around 3 to 5 percent of the workforce is unemployed.

Unfortunately, unemployment is a constant in our economy. The Bureau of Labor Statistics keeps track of joblessness in different age groups, races, and genders. Several different types of unemployment have been identified by economists:

- **Structural**—This happens when certain industries become obsolete. Workers with certain skills have no place to go.
- **Seasonal—**Landscapers, farmers, and certain tourism jobs are tossed out of work at certain downtimes during the year.
- **Frictional**—These are people who are just entering the job market or those who have decided to leave to seek out "greener pastures." This is the largest segment of the overall unemployment figure during periods of strong economic growth and high employment.
- **Cyclical**—Certain industries are hit hard by downturns in the economy. Auto workers are typically laid off during recessions as they wait for consumers to buy more of their companies' products.

As you can see, there will always be some unemployment, even in the most productive of economies. At between 4 and 5 percent, many economists consider us to be at full employment right now. In other words, despite the natural occurrences of situations just mentioned, we are at **full employment** when rates are that low.

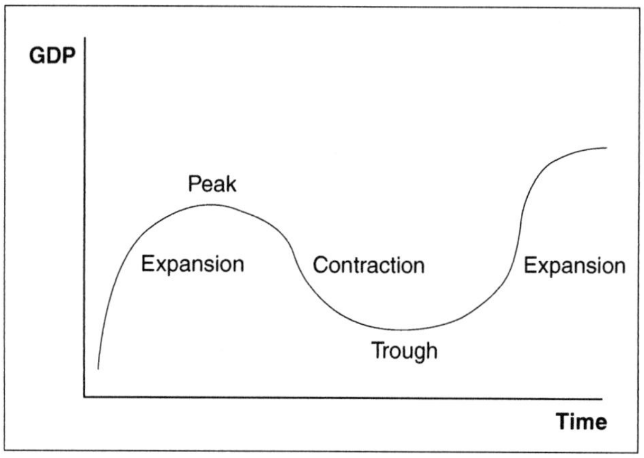

The Pressing Questions

13. High unemployment affects all of society. What do you think the three biggest social effects of joblessness are?

14. Create a definition for *recession.*

Unemployment Rates			
1950	4.3	1990	6.3
1955	4.2	1991	7.3
1960	6.6	1992	7.4
1965	4.0	1993	6.5
1970	6.1	1994	5.5
1975	8.2	1995	5.6
1980	7.2	1996	5.4
1982	10.2	1997	4.7
1984	7.3	1998	4.3
1986	6.6	1999	4.4
1988	6.3	2000	

Source: Bureau of Labor Statistics

I. Inflation Is Bad News

Some may say that these words are a bit harsh and out of place in an economics discussion. One thing remains sure: inflation will destroy the strongest of economies. It is by far the worst (potential) problem we face as a nation. Because of its damaging effects, our government, especially the Federal Reserve, watches for its slightest signs.

Simply enough, inflation is an increase in the average price level for goods and services across an economy. Let's say that the price of tires is rising rapidly. Perhaps there is a rubber shortage causing the increase, or maybe people are simply buying a lot of radials. Both of these situations can cause a price increase.

A rise in the cost of one product is not a problem for the United States as a whole. But what if the price of tires, groceries, toys, wood, cars, steel—and everything else for that matter—were on the rise? Families would have a harder time living within their budget. Even worse, companies would have a difficult time planning for the future. No one could predict next year's prices. Consumers would get nervous, and corporations would stop hiring and buying equipment. People tend to spend their money more vigorously in an inflationary economy, because they are afraid that their money will lose value.

For instance, in the late 1970s, annual prices were increasing at a rate of 13 percent per year. That means that a car that cost $10,000 this year will cost $11,300 next year. A $100 dollar grocery order will increase by another $13. Because bank interest rates take time to keep up with such devaluation of the dollar, saving becomes less and less common for the consumer. People simply want to spend before their money loses any more value, especially for big-ticket items like cars and appliances.

This rapid spending prompts retailers to continue to raise prices in the face of the consumer frenzy. All in all, inflation creates more inflation. People realize that prices are increasing and respond by spending their money more quickly. This prompts producers to raise prices, thus creating more inflation. Inflation should always be nipped in the bud. If the powers that be notice that the Consumer Price Index (CPI) and other indicators rose from 1.5 to 1.8 percent, they would take measures to stop the trend. To put it simply, inflation breeds more inflation. Once it gets started, it is most difficult to stop it.

Consumer Price Index			
1915	10.1	1985	107.6
1920	20	1990	130.7
1925	17.5	1991	136.2
1930	16.7	1992	140.3
1940	13.7	1993	144.5
1945	14	1994	148.2
1950	24.1	1995	152.4
1960	26.8	1996	156.9
1965	31.5	1997	160.5
1970	38.8	1998	163
1975	53.8	1999	167.1
1980	82.4	2000	

Source: Bureau of Labor Statistics

When prices reach a high enough point, consumers, tired of their wages not keeping up with the rising prices, may decide to stop buying all together to wait out the storm. The result will be a severe slowdown of the economy.

The lack of sales will force factories to shut their doors and existing companies to curtail production. When that happens, jobs will soon be lost. The potential result of even a minor bout with inflation is a serious and prolonged depression where the consumer is too afraid to spend any money.

Inflation has two ways of getting started. It can come from the supply of our economy or the demand:

- **Supply-side inflation** occurs when the resource prices in our economy go up for various reasons. These increased prices can force up the cost of other consumer and producer goods. For instance, in the mid-1970s, OPEC countries imposed an embargo on the United States. The price of a barrel more than doubled forcing the prices of every product in our country.
- **Demand-side inflation** comes from people buying too many goods. In essence, there are too many dollars chasing too few goods. Our producers cannot keep up with consumer demand, and they raise the prices.

But how do we keep people from buying things? And wasn't a hot economy a good thing? Using statistics kept by the government, economists keep a close eye on how much people are buying (**aggregate demand**) and how much factories are producing (**aggregate supply**). These statistics are vital to our future growth as a nation.

The Pressing Question

15. Another dilemma that comes from inflation is called the wage-price spiral. Draw a representation of one below.

J. Watching Inflation Closely

For the past several years, our national rate of inflation has been around 1.5 to 3 percent per year. The Bureau of Labor Statistics (a branch of the Labor Department) publishes two figures every month that are closely watched by all interested in the health of our economy.

- **Consumer Price Index** (CPI)—this refers to a sample of 80,000 of the most commonly bought consumer goods from rental housing, utilities, food, clothes, entertainment, and health care. The total is compared to a base year (currently 1984), and a number of figures are calculated for various regions around the country.
- **Producer Price Index** (PPI)—This measures the different prices of goods at all stages of the production process. The figures are also compared to a base year, but a tally of products is kept. Various categories like agricultural, processed food, and fuels are kept.

When inflation occurs, a worker has to earn more money to keep the same standard of living that he or she had last year. Because inflation will cause a rise in the price of most goods and services, it will simply cost more to run a household. Professions have to keep up with inflation by offering workers **cost of living increases**. Many labor contracts and government programs like social security are directly tied to the **cost of living adjustment** figures provided by the CPI.

The Pressing Questions

16. If the CPI was 100 in 1983, and a leather couch cost $650 at that time, how much would that couch cost today with the CPI at 165 if the price of the couch increased at the same rate as the inflation rate?

17. If the CPI was 155.2 in 1995 and 149.9 in 1994, what was the rate of inflation (in percentage terms) for 1994–1995?

The moves of the Federal Reserve are watched closely by anyone who has or deals with money.

K. More Details on Inflation

It has been mentioned before that once inflation starts, it is very difficult to stop. One major cause of this is due to a situation called the **wage-price spiral**. When prices begin to rise, workers will begin to demand higher wages. Suppliers can do this only if demand is strong enough to allow them to do so. If workers eventually get the extra money, they will tend to spend that quickly if they believe that prices will continue to rise. Store owners will notice the increased sales or the higher labor costs and then raise prices even more. This is why it is vital to catch inflation before it starts.

If inflation is left unchecked, people will eventually be unable to afford any products. Banks will raise interest rates higher to ensure profits. With inflation of 13 percent in 1980, banks offered rates on home mortgages of almost 20 percent. This brought the construction and car industries to their respective knees. Nobody liked the prospect of paying the interest that came with an inflationary economy.

The worst case scenario comes when the government ignores the warning signs like a rising CPI and product shortages. If inflation is left completely unchecked and the money supply continues to grow too quickly, prices can rise most rapidly. For example, Germany in the 1920s printed billions of marks to pay back other countries for the reparations demanded in the Versailles Treaty. Markets responded to the flood of cheap money by jacking up prices to unbelievable heights.

Imagine that this week when you buy a loaf of bread, it costs $1.00. When you go shopping next week, you are amazed to find that the price has risen to $50.00. People had to carry baskets full of money just to buy their daily bread. This **hyperinflation** eroded the confidence the German people had in their government. Their society had to deal with the chaos. This is one of the reasons that Hitler rose to power.

Quite the opposite of inflation, **deflation** is a condition where the average prices for goods and services fall across an economy. In the late 1800s, farmers who were already hit hard by plummeting prices due to automation, also had to deal with a gold-backed currency that steadily increased in value (because the growth of the money supply did not keep up with the growth of the economy). Their crop prices fell even further. When they needed to borrow money to save their farms, banks—noticing the scarcity of money—raised interest rates as high as 80 percent. Today, for many reasons, we prefer a controlled amount of inflation around 1 to 3 percent. Don't confuse deflation with a situation called **disinflation**. Disinflation is when the rate of inflation falls from a higher rate to a lower rate without becoming deflationary. When inflation rates fell from 13 percent in 1980 to 4 percent in 1985, it was said that the dollar was "disinflating."

What if the unemployment that usually comes with a severe period of inflation continues for a prolonged period of time? We are then stuck with high inflation *and* high unemployment, called **stagflation**. It is difficult to envision a worse scenario. In the early 1970s, spending on the Vietnam War and social programs were financed with an increase in the money supply. When oil prices shot up from $1/barrel in 1970 to $35 in 1982, prices shot up further and businesses cut back production because resource prices were cutting into profits.

As you can probably see, inflation is a problem that is best dealt with swiftly and surely. The economic health of our country depends upon the actions of our government. In the United States, much of the job of keeping the specter of inflation in chains is the Federal Reserve's.

The Pressing Question

18. If inflation is so bad, list four of the negative impacts.

L. Origins of the Federal Reserve

Those farmers that we talked about in the previous section raised awareness in the United States to the need for monetary policy. In addition to the Populist movement, a financial crisis in 1907 left the nation's banking structure teetering on the brink of disaster. People looked to the government to save the economy, but there were no provisions or agencies to handle the situation.

All appeared lost until a private citizen, J. P. Morgan, agreed to float the largest banks massive loans. We were saved by someone in the private sector. But what if he didn't feel like lending a hand?

That is why, in 1911, Congress passed the **Federal Reserve Act** and thus established our national bank. They wanted it to keep a close eye on our money supply and **issue** more money in times of financial strain. The leaders of the Federal Reserve are the watchdogs that protect us from the two worst problems we face as a nation—inflation and recession. To do this, they watch for signs of both very closely.

The idea of central banking goes back to the very beginning of our nation. Some of the founding fathers who tended to be more conservative feared putting all financial power into the hands of the federal government. Other men, like **Alexander Hamilton**, believed that it was vital to our young nation that a central bank lead our economic growth and competition with foreign countries. The national bank was given a shaky beginning and only lasted until 1834 when Andrew Jackson vetoed the renewal of its charter. Not until 1911 did the United States again establish a national bank.

Not only did the incident in 1907 with J. P. Morgan convince the Congress of our need for a national bank, but also the traumatic economic events of the 1800s had a part in our moving towards centralization. Frequent depressions, then called "panics," occurred in 1813, 1837, 1857, 1873, 1884, and 1893. During these events, there would be massive unemployment and stagnant growth in our national product. To make things worse, the banking system would begin to crumble. Small banks relied on big banks to hold their capital. When the small banks got scared, they would withdraw their money from the big bank. Depositors would respond by requesting their money as well. This pyramidal reserve system would quickly collapse. With many people losing their money, there truly was a sense of panic in the air.

Because businesses need access to capital to grow, there would be little chance for economic growth when the banks could not lend out any money. While finding capital is no problem during the good times, it makes recovery from a bad economy more difficult. Even worse, panicked depositors would literally run to their local banks to withdraw their savings. Often this escalated into a full-scale "panic." The tension that consumers felt caused a severe drop in sales and thus production. The economy suffered. And with little or no cash around, prospects would appear dim.

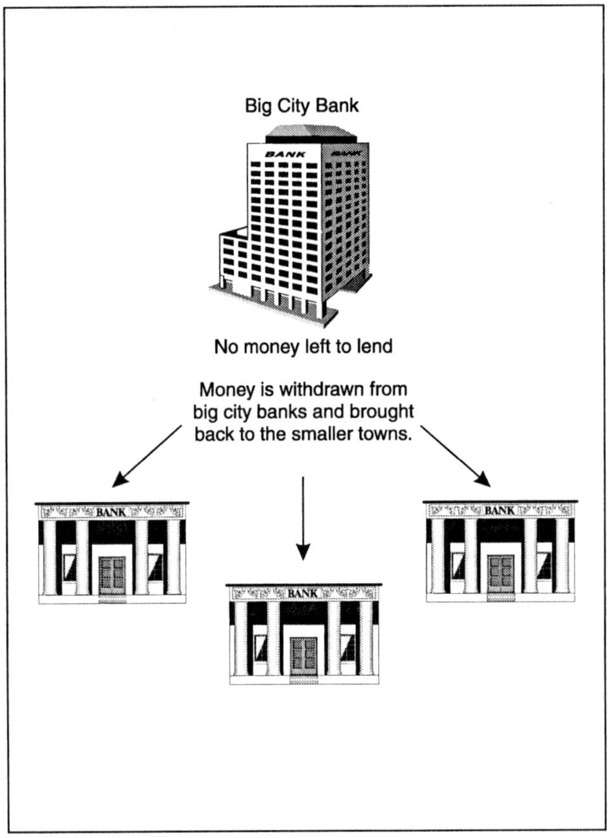

The Pressing Question

19. After considering the problems that faced the United States, what three powers would you give to the a national bank to help prevent such dilemmas?

M. Structure of the Federal Reserve

If you have a dollar bill handy, take it out and look at it. On the front side at the top is the writing, "Federal Reserve Note." This means that the Fed, as it is called, issues each piece of currency that we handle in the United States. Contrary to popular belief, however, the Fed does not print the money. Creating money is the job of the U.S Treasury and the U.S. Mint.

On the front of the bill, to the left of George Washington, there will be a letter from A through

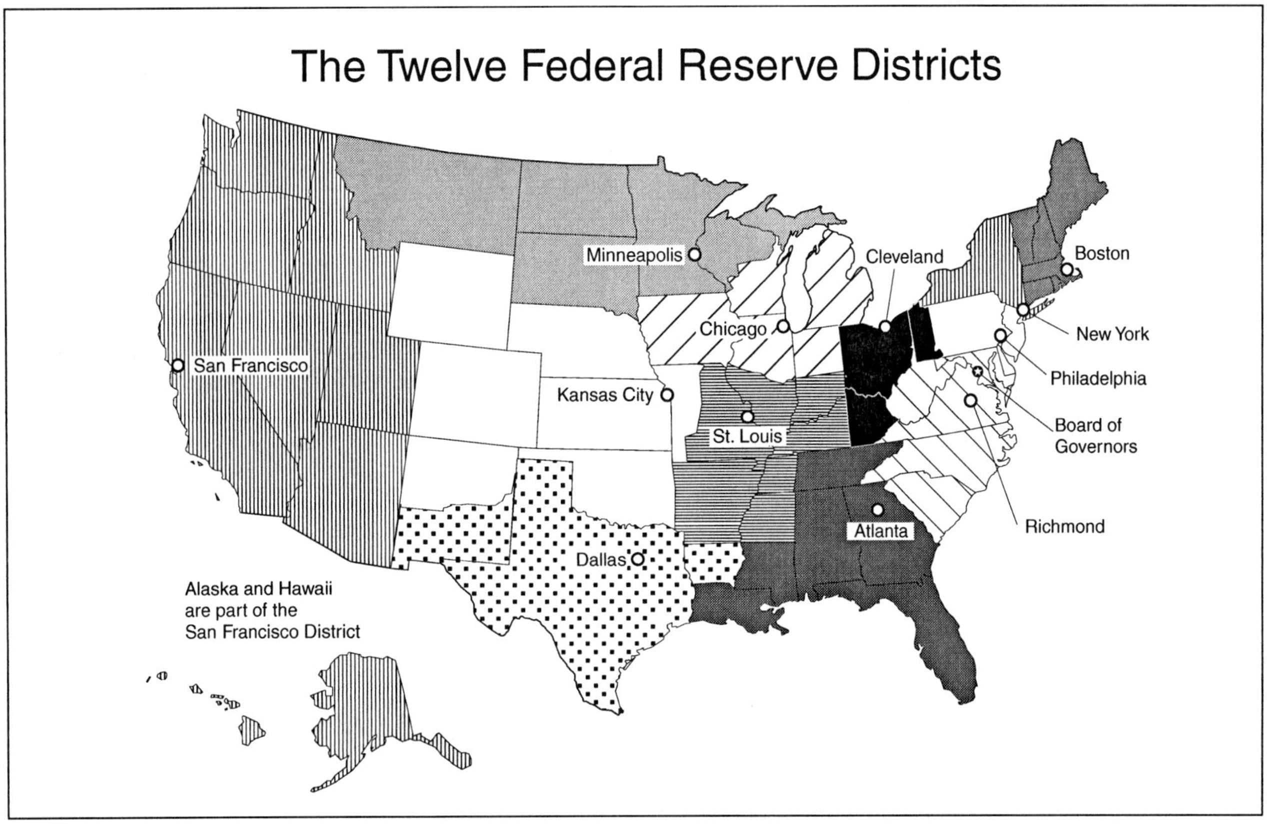

L. Each of those letters represents one of the twelve districts of the Federal Reserve System. If you have a bill from Cleveland, for instance, the letter in the seal will be D.

The hierarchy of the Fed is headed by one person, the Chairman of the **Board of Governors**. This board has seven members and meets with the presidents of the twelve branch banks about once a month in a body called the **Federal Open Market Committee** (FOMC). They pour over tens of thousands of pieces of data from around the country, including reports from each of the presidents, who also meet with representatives of their local business community. When their decisions are made, the Fed Chairman must report to Congress about once per quarter to explain its actions. To put it simply, the Federal Reserve is independent within the government.

Also a part of the system are the 5,900 member banks. These commercial banks have to follow strict guidelines passed by the Fed. Furthermore, they must face a yearly audit or examination from inspectors who want to determine the health or **solvency** of the bank.

The Pressing Question

20. If you were a bank examiner, what factors do you think would be most important to prove the health of a bank?

N. The Fed in Action

The Fed is responsible for fighting two major problems: inflation and recessions. The worse is inflation. However, significant slumps in the economy are painful to society as a whole. The goal of **monetary policy** is to allow for steady economic growth while making sure the economy does not get "too hot" and fall into a period of inflation.

First of all, the Fed, in cooperation with the Treasury Department, collects all of the government's money and pays all of its bills. The IRS collects the four trillion dollars in tax revenue, and the Secretary of the Treasury keeps measure of all of the outlays of cash to the government programs and creditors while the Fed helps keep track as the holder of the Treasury's checking account.

In order to watch the economy more carefully, the Fed employs economists who watch production levels very closely. They want to know exactly what prices are and how much companies are producing. To judge where the economy might be going in the next six to twelve months, an index is kept to watch eleven figures that make up our **Leading Economic Indicators**. They are as follows:

- average work week
- new claims for unemployment
- new orders for goods
- vendor performance
- contracts and orders for new equipment
- new building permits
- changes in unfilled manufacturing orders
- changes in sensitive material prices
- stock indexes
- M2
- consumer expectations

In addition to all of these, GDP, the CPI, the PPI, and the trade deficit are also tracked. Sometimes housing starts, or the amount of new home construction, give a good indication of where the economy is headed.

The Fed has many weapons in its arsenal. With all of this power comes the awesome responsibility of using the power wisely and judiciously. Some of the Fed's functions are as follows:

- Supervising member banks—If a bank wants to keep or borrow money with the central bank, it must abide by the Fed's rules and audits.
- Monitoring money—Cash is recycled and issued through the twelve member banks.
- Lender of last resort—When a bank gets in real trouble and no one else wants to lend it money, the Fed can step in.

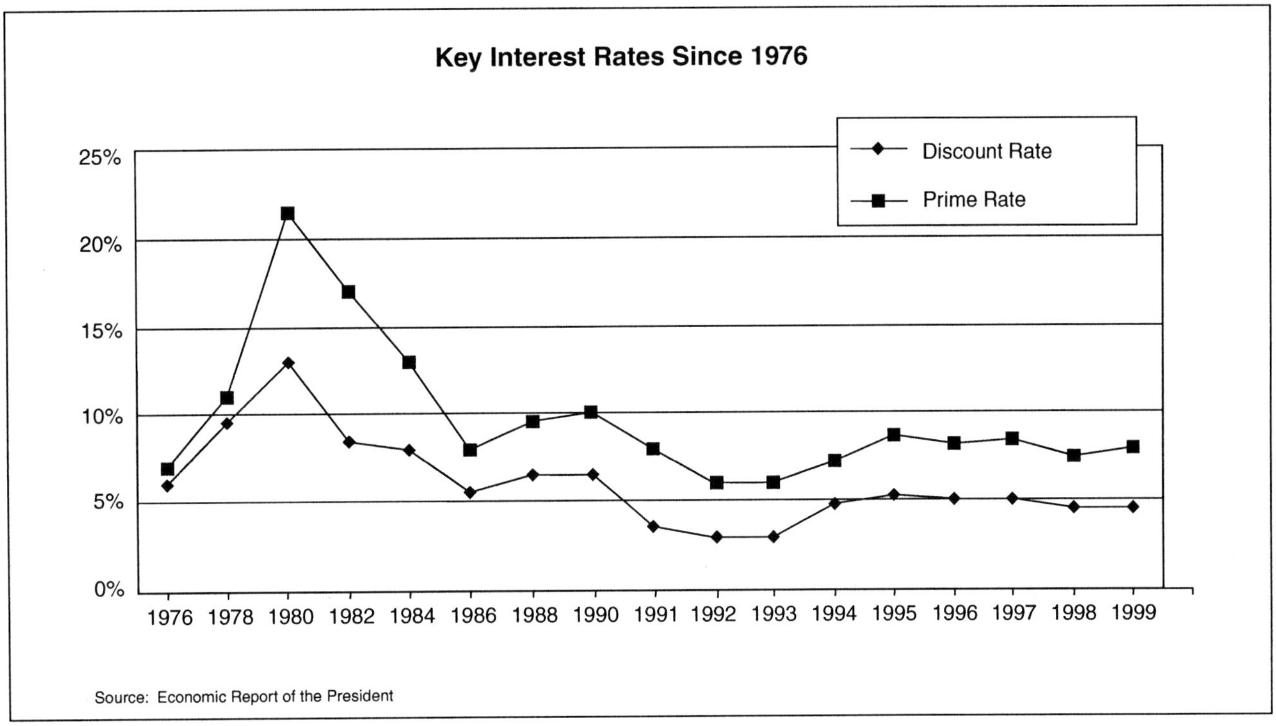

- Regulating the money supply—The amount of money that is available can affect the rate of inflation and interest rates. Like it does for banks, the Fed is a source of money for the whole economy.
- Moral persuasion—The Chairman has the most powerful vocabulary in the world. His words can shake markets when he believes that people are not behaving responsibly.
- Setting interest rates—This is the most visible of all the Fed's jobs. The **discount rate** (the rate that banks pay when they borrow from the Fed) affects the **prime rate** (the rate that banks give to their best customers) which will in turn affect the rates that we are offered by banks.
- Setting the reserve requirement—Member banks are required to keep a certain amount of a depositor's savings as cash. The rest of it can be lent back out. In other words, if you deposit $1000, and the reserve requirement is 15 percent, then the bank must keep $150 in the vaults. The other $850 does not stay in the bank. It gets invested or lent out again.
- Check clearing—Every check written in the United States must go from one bank to another. These are physically scanned and cleared by the district Fed bank. This task is also shared with some private clearing houses.

The Federal Reserve's decisions have an enormous impact on foreign economies. With the introduction of the euro as a means of electronic exchange in 1999, the future of American money will rest with the Treasury and the Fed.

These tools can speed up the economy or bring it to a screeching halt. But, when used wisely, they can produce years of steady growth. This means that prosperity can be more evenly spread to all Americans.

The Pressing Question

21. What do you think is happening if the following figures are published in the paper?
    a. housing starts up 15 percent

    b. CPI falls from 4 to 2 percent

    c. new claims for unemployment up 8 percent

O. How Do They Do That?

Let's say that the economy is in a slump. Prices don't seem to be rising, but the unemployment rate has gone from 5.2 percent to 8.5 percent. People and businesses are beginning to worry that the situation will get worse. Consumers are not buying, so the businesses are forced to cut production resulting in massive job losses. Not to worry though, there is a way to get the people back into the stores. The secret is to help them save money. One way to do that is to cut interest rates. An even easier and more direct way is to increase the money supply. This has the effect of lowering interest rates and stimulating the demand for goods and services as people spend their excess cash balances.

For instance, if someone wants to build a house for $200,000 at 12 percent, it will cost them about $2,500 per month on a thirty-year mortgage. That is out of the price range of many people. If the rates fell to 7 percent, they could build the same house for around 1,500 per month. It could be the same for the purchase of houses, cars, new factories, or heavy equipment. Interest rates can impact the economy in significant ways.

The Fed can lower rates by lowering the **discount rate**. Being the lender of last resort, they lend to banks that have exhausted all other credit options. These short-term loans help a bank maintain cash reserves. The Fed also controls the Federal Funds Rate, or the rate at which banks lend to other banks. This target number is hit by the Fed's periodic adjustment of the money supply. The prime rate, or the rate that banks offer to other banks and big businesses, will nudge up or down in response to the fluctuations in the discount and federal funds.

The availability of money around the economy can also alert banks as to what to do about commercial interest rates. Banks are just like any other business. If a shoe store has too many shoes piling up in the store room, they will have to have a sale. It is the same thing with a bank. If there is too much cash piling up in the vaults, the banks will be prompted to have a "sale." Since the cost of borrowing money is interest, they will drop their own interest rates. Lower interest rates might cause more buying (producers may be tempted to raise prices), and inflation might creep up on us.

One of the things that the Fed will do when the first signs of inflation appear will be to curtail the growth of the money supply. The contraction and expansion of the money supply is done through an activity called **open market operations.** M1 and M2 are constantly monitored for changes. And because money cannot simply be given away, the Fed buys and sells bonds. Here is how it works:

- **Increase the money supply**—The FOMC will buy bonds from investors with cash from its own vaults. The money will end up in banks which will then lend the money to producers and consumers.
- **Decrease the money supply**—The Fed will sell bonds from its vast holdings to the bond markets. This will draw money from banks' reserves; thus, there will be less money to lend to producers and consumers.

Again, businesses need easy access to capital to grow and prosper. But too much cash in the hands of banks and consumers can cause a rise in inflation.

Remember that the Fed has two huge weapons against inflation and recessions.

- **Easy-money policy**—Increase the money supply, and lower the discount rate
- **Tight-money policy**—Decrease the money supply, and raise the discount rate

If there is a slowdown in the economy, then the Fed will counter with an easy-money policy. This will prompt businesses and consumers to spend more freely. On the other hand, if things get too "hot," they can be cooled off with a tight-money supply. Against these two main foes, the Fed is very effective.

There are limitations to monetary policy. First of all, markets are slow to react to stimuli, and these time lags can take from six to eighteen months to pass. Second, many people feel that the Fed has too much power. People called **monetarists** believe that all the Fed should do is let the money supply grow slowly and not respond to the temporary fluctuations in the economy with the discount rate. Third, the Fed has no control over the actions of Congress, and many times, the big spending and low taxes of a generous government can contradict the stringent measures of a more disciplined Fed.

The 1990s has been the most prosperous and productive decade in U.S. history. While some attribute good economies to the Congress or president, it is more likely that the Federal Reserve has had the most impact.

Nation	GDP	Per Capita GDP	Real Growth (%)	Unemployment	Inflation
United States	8.3 tr	30,270	3.5	4.3	1.5
China	3.4 tr	2,802	9.7	0.0	10
Japan	2.8 tr	22,718	1.6	3.4	.3
Germany	1.7 tr	20,350	1.4	10.8	1.5
India	1.5 tr	1,615	6.5	NA	10.3
France	1.2 tr	20,920	1.3	12.7	1.7
U.K.	1.19 tr	20,345	2.4	6.7	2.6
Italy	1.12 tr	19,492	0.8	12	4.0
Brazil	1.02 tr	6,283	2.9	5.2	10
Indonesia	780 bil	3,774	7.0	3.0	7.0

Source: Statistical Abstract of the United States

The last problem is much more serious. It is called **stagflation**. In the late 1970s, high inflation and high unemployment forced then-Chair of the Fed Paul Volcker to choose one of the problems to fight. He and the FOMC decided that inflation was much worse and raised interest rates. The prime rate reached a high of 21 percent. The money supply slowed in its growth, and cash became hard to come by. Businesses were unable to borrow for expansion. Consumer spending slowed to a snail's pace. By 1983, however, the lack of spending forced producers to lower their prices and inflation fell back to reasonable areas. The United States had to endure the high interest rates and shrunken money supply that were required to battle inflation. The cost in the meantime was an unemployment rate that topped out in 1980 at 13 percent.

The Fed's powers have allowed the United States to experience an unprecedented period of steady growth. During the 1990s, inflation was low, unemployment was low, and people felt confident about the future. We, as a country, have never experienced such continuous growth. In the 1800s, we would boom, become inflationary, then bust. Today, economists are arguing about how long we can sustain growth without experiencing our next recession. How long do you think we will continue to grow?

The Pressing Question

22. Write in a policy that the Fed would use against the following:

    a. inflation

    b. high unemployment

    c. stagflation

    d. slow economy

    e. hot economy

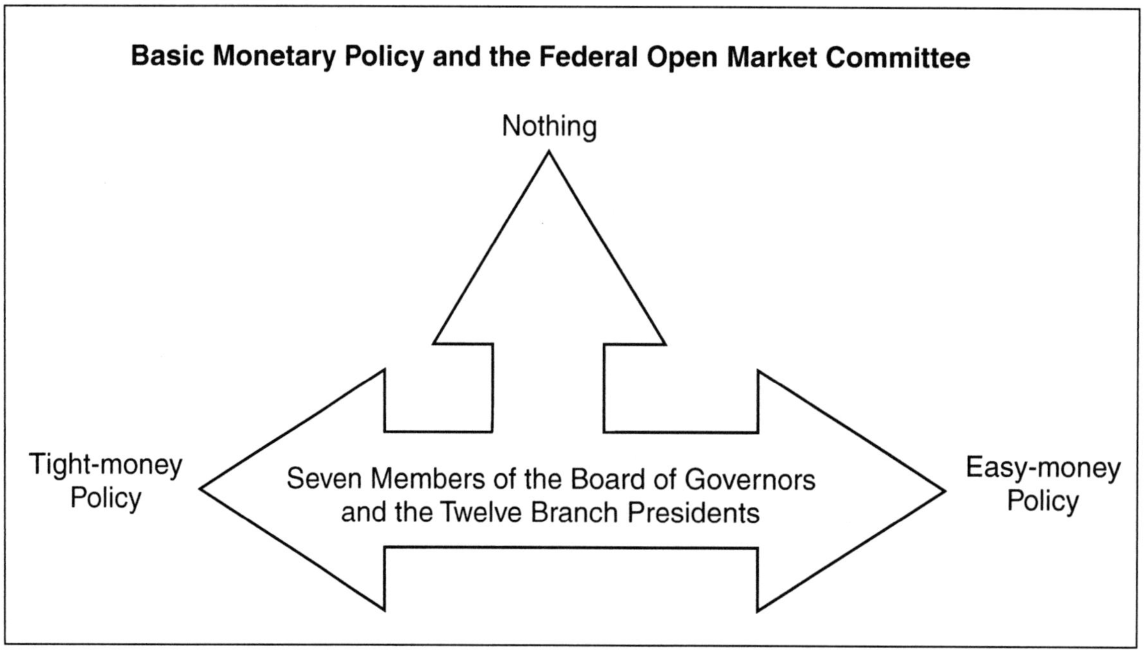

Name________________________

Date________________________

Reading and Vocabulary

Directions: Write the appropriate answers in the blanks provided. Then circle those answers in the word find.

________________ 1. He led the Federal Reserve during the "war on inflation" in the early 1980s.

________________ 2. He led the Federal Reserve in the boom years of the 1990s.

________________ 3. _____ persuasion is the use of words to cajole more appropriate behavior.

________________ 4. to exchange goods without the use of money

________________ 5. gold or silver currency

________________ 6. Our money today is known as _____ money.

________________ 7. the first people in the world to coin money

________________ 8. His law stated that "bad money will always drive out the good money."

________________ 9. the amount of money borrowed in a loan

________________ 10. the cost of using someone else's money

________________ 11. the agency that insures your bank deposits to $100,000

________________ 12. the lowest interest rate set by the Fed

________________ 13. the number of districts in the Federal Reserve System

________________ 14. Overall, prices are rising steadily.

________________ 15. Money that consisted of shells or other trinkets is known as ____ money.

________________ 16. The rate that is given by banks to its best customers is known as the _____ rate.

________________ 17. Inflation fell from 5 percent to 1 percent.

________________ 18. Inflation rose to 500 percent in less than a year.

________________ 19. The Fed is the "_______ of last resort."

________________ 20. main decision making body of the Federal Reserve (abbreviation)

________________ 21. main gauge for measuring consumer prices (abbreviation)

________________ 22. a slump in the economy

________________ 23. C + I + G + F = ? (abbreviation)

________________ 24. agency in charge of investigating counterfeiters

________________ 25. Money used during the gold standard was known as ______ money.

________________ 26. Policy formulated by the Federal Reserve is known as ______ policy.

Name________________________

Date________________________

R P C D I S I N F L A T I O N M F O M C X Z A P O P Y U T U

E L K J E S O H D Y B V B X Q O E A O X B M L P T R N K L E

C G F D E T U O M N H G Y R I P L E D C X X M I H I U I O J

E C F R S E F V B N R E P R S E N T A T I V E U Y N F R D K

S K G M D T Y O P F D R E B N K P F G H J D G J K C H U F D

S G J O J J O P E W D V N J U G E G H J J K D E S I D H J C

I H I N T E R E S T D N C T G R E E N S P A N C B P B X V P

O V C E N J F S F T G H S F G O P D S G J Y J E O A K L E I

N C D T G H T L H S F C V B M H Y U K D G H J F D L S V N N

C B O A I H L E J L U G R E S H A M P O M F Y D N J K F D Y

H U K R V D J N F O U I L L G L R J I F O F D I S C O U N T

F J I Y K Y F D J D M M K D V J D E X D N J C C X H U S X B

L O R J V K S E C R E T S E R V I C E V E H G B C K Y D C J

J C T Y O P G R K I K B F H D G N J I F T F R G V N K S G U

J D P L L C D S A X D F E X Z S F F S W A V X V V Z C P O I

B A R T E R K J Y H G F D S C S L A S D R G H O H J K E I Z

P O I I N B Y T D G H J H F D G A D E E Y X V L V C D C P O

K L M J C O M M O D I T Y H G V T F D D D D X C X V S I P T

G H E H J N B V C D E W Q A S F I A T X C V B K B H F E F W

D X Z S O X V G V T B N K O H V O I U G J D H E C N M K D E

D H K G G L Y D I A N S J L D X N B N M C M O R A L X E R L

S V N B G B J F G Y H U H U I O E A S F S F D H J D Y I N V

G H D N D V H M L O H F H Y P E R I N F L A T I O N M J L E

V J O K P K I B H E S S K J I N F L I T I Y N R E X H J H I

Name____________________________

Date____________________________

Mind on Your Money

Directions: With the help of your reading, an almanac, or a recent newspaper, fill in the chart. When finished, answer the questions.

Country	Name of Currency	$100 in Their Currency
Germany		
Great Britain		
Italy		
Spain		
Australia		
Japan		
Canada		
Russia		
China		
Brazil		
Mexico		
European Community		

1. What does it mean when the dollar gets stronger? weaker?

2. List four countries whose currency is also called a dollar.

Name______________________

Date______________________

3. If you are planning to go to France this summer, do you want the dollar to weaken or strengthen? Give an example that you can present in class.

4. When the Japanese yen weakened in the early 1990s, how did it affect the prices of American products in Tokyo?

5. Explain whether you think it is better to have a strong or weak dollar.

6. What role is the new euro currency playing in our global economy?

Name________________________

Date________________________

You and the CPI

Part A.

Directions: Using the formula provided, figure out what the following products and services *should* cost in today's dollars. Use a simple algebraic ratio to find the cost in today's dollars. Then, in the next column, jot down what they actually cost in today's dollars. Then, in the next column, jot down what they *actually* cost. You may consult other people or sources if you are unsure of a price. The current CPI is ______________.

Product	Year	Old Price	Old Year CPI	It Should Cost	It Actually Costs	Explanation
1. Three-bedroom house	1946	$10,000	19			
2. Loaf of bread, pound of butter, gallon of milk, and a pound of ground beef	1940	$4.16	14.1			
3. Cheap seat at a major-league baseball game	1960	$1.00	29.5			
4. Movie ticket	1975	$2.00	53			
5. One year at state college	1965	$400	31.6			
6. VCR	1978	$875	74			
7. CD player	1985	$750	108			
8. Apple IIe computer	1980	$1600	82			
9. Average annual income of a high school graduate	1940	$1500	14.1			
10. Model T Ford (use a modern equivalent)	1925	$525	18			

Part B.

Directions: For each of the following years, calculate the percent change from year to year. That is the rate of inflation.

Rates of Inflation

Year	1990	1991	1992	1993	1994	1995	1996	1997	1998	1999	2000
CPI	129.9	136	140.2	144.4	149.9	155.2	157	160	163	166.4	
% Change		4.5%									

Name________________________

Date________________________

Part C.

Directions: Answer the following questions.

1. Which products are more expensive than they used to be? Which ones are cheaper?

2. How can things like food actually go down in price over time?

3. Why do high-tech products like VCRs go down in price so much?

4. How could you describe the rates of inflation in the 1990s? Is this good or bad?

Name_________________________

Date_________________________

Basic Monetary Policy

Part A.

Directions: For each of the following terms and phrases, provide a definition.

1. Time lag

2. Hot economy

3. Three indicators of inflation

4. Disinflation

5. Three indicators of recession

6. A downturn in the economy

7. An economic slump

8. The economy is cooling off

9. Unemployment

10. Productivity

11. Leading economic indicators

12. Stagflation

Name_______________________

Date_______________________

Part B.

Directions: Fill in the following chart.

Action Taken by the Fed	Desired Result
1. Raise interest rates	
2. Tighten the money supply	
3. Lower interest rates	
4. Easy-money policy	
5. Raise the reserve requirement	
6. Loosen the money supply	
7. Take over a bank	
8. Tight-money policy	
9. Warn the public of inflation	
10. Audit a bank	
11. Leave interest rates alone	

Name________________________

Date________________________

Monetary Policy in Action

Directions: Each of the following scenarios calls for a certain course of action. In the column marked "Fed Action," choose easy-money policy, tight-money policy, moral persuasion, or nothing. If you need to review what those choices actually are, refer to your reading. Remember, what the FOMC decides will have an impact on all of us. They do not make their decisions lightly!

Economic Problem	Fed Action	Anticipated Result
1. Stock prices have declined for the last two weeks.		
2. GNP dipped from 3 percent to 1 percent in the last year.		
3. The CPI and PPI have risen 3 percent in the last six months.		
4. Commercial interest rates are rising, but the Fed has not raised rates.		
5. The prices of cars have tripled in the last year.		
6. GNP is growing steadily, and prices are rising sharply.		
7. The United States is experiencing both high inflation and high unemployment.		
8. The CPI is up, and housing starts are at a fifteen-year high.		
9. We are in a recession. Factory orders are down, and the economy appears to be slumping.		
10. Consumers feel worried, inflation is low, and spending is sluggish.		
11. Unemployment is low, and prices are rising steadily.		
12. The index of leading economic indicators shows a strong move towards inflation.		
13. The Fed senses that people are not saving enough money.		
14. Jobless rates are pushing 11 percent while the CPI has fallen from 8 percent to 2 percent growth.		
15. We are in a recession but are experiencing high inflation.		
16. The money supply appears to be tight, and prices are on the rise.		
17. Prices are stable, and the GDP is growing at a 3 percent pace.		

Name______________________

Date______________________

The Chairman of the Fed Speaks

Directions: For years since the beginning of the 1990s, the stock market has enjoyed the greatest prosperity ever. Investments have tripled in value, but this can sometimes have an adverse economic effect. Alan Greenspan had something to say about the runaway bull market. Read the following article, and then answer the questions in full sentences.

All over the world, from Wall Street to Main Street, the financial world was buzzing about what Alan Greenspan said the other night. Nobody knew that two little words could have such an impact on the world's financial markets.

In the last few months of last year, the chair of the Fed apparently shot from the hip and let the stock market have it. Again, while addressing a dinner engagement, he said, "How do we know when irrational exuberance has unduly escalated asset values, which then become subject to unexpected and prolonged contractions as they have had in Japan in the last decade?" Then the trouble began.

As Asian markets opened, the word of Greenspan's doom hit the streets. Panicked investors sold off their parts of their portfolios sending the major markets of the east into a tailspin. Europe did the same. By the time that New York opened for trading, it seemed all wanted to sell and the market fell 144 points as a result. The words "irrational exuberance" echoed over the trading pits.

Investors didn't seem to care much about Greenspan's feeling about stock prices, but they did seem to worry about a possible shift in the way the Fed handles monetary decisions in the future.

With the influx of money into the stock markets, does Greenspan worry about declining savings rates? Would he prefer to see a more traditional means of saving for retirement make a comeback in the United States? It is hard to say, but in any case, this man is listened to.

In later speeches, the Fed Chairman has used words like "caution," and "questions of sustainability." Considering that this man has considerable influence inside the secretive halls of the FOMC, glimpses like these are always heeded and obeyed. The market took weeks to recover.

Economists from across the globe are left scratching their heads. It is not like Greenspan to meddle in the affairs of the stock market. Nor does he take his cryptic words lightly. He definitely has something up his sleeve, let's hope his next trick doesn't cost the world a few billion dollars like his last one did.

1. Using a dictionary, define the phrase *irrational exuberance.*

2. What did Alan Greenspan mean by describing the market that way?

Name________________________

Date________________________

3. What power of the Fed was he using by speaking those words?

4. What impact could Greenspan and the FOMC have on the stock market?

5. What types of companies could be most affected by his decisions?

6. How did world and domestic markets react to his words?

7. What is Greenspan worried about if he believes he should use these words?

8. Would monetary policy be better served by having Congress handle it?

9. What impact did other stock market crashes have on the economy?

Part 4
Government and the Economy

Questions to Consider

1. Do you consider yourself to be a conservative or a liberal?
2. Are you a Democrat or a Republican?
3. What basic economic rights do you have?
4. How involved is our government with the economy?
5. How effective is our government?
6. How big is our government?
7. How much does our government spend?
8. How much does our government tax us?

Terms You Need in Order to Read

Conservative	Deficit	Regulation
Liberal	Federalism	Fiscal policy
Debt		

Name________________________

Date________________________

Government and the Economy

Directions: Read the selection, and answer the Pressing Questions as you read. Be prepared for class discussion.

A. Where Do You Stand?

From the very beginning of our country's history, there has been an endless debate about the government's involvement in the economy. You may recall from your American history class two groups of people called the Federalists and Antifederalists. Some people believed that the federal (national) government should remain small and rarely interfere with the economy. Others believed that it was in our national interest that the government get directly involved with our economic affairs. The argument between the two factions is at the heart of our political system.

The **Antifederalists**, led by **Thomas Jefferson,** had a fundamental distrust of any government. Having just ousted an obtrusive monarchy from England, they were not anxious to let another government start taxing them and telling them how to live. Their conservative beliefs are still around today in the Republican party. Economically, the modern **conservative** seeks lower taxes, less spending by the federal government, more power to the state governments, and less regulations placed upon business.

The Federalists, led by **Alexander Hamilton**, believed that the federal government, not the states, should monitor and engineer the growth of the economy. They wanted to see the United States develop as an industrial complex and compete with Europe. Because they advocated a strong central power, and a change from things in the past, the **Federalists** were very liberal for their day. Today, **liberals** advocate stringent control of business by government and choose to defer power to the federal rather than state governments. Lastly, liberals today believe that the federal government should use its power to alleviate social problems that our society faces.

If you already have some political opinions, it is important that you clarify them as you read this section. Many of the ideas are controversial, and some may even anger you. Try to be open to new ideas, but also be firm in what you hold most dear. We live together in the oldest democracy human beings have ever seen. The ability of our government to function is vital to the health of our society. Because you are a citizen, you must take part in determining the direction in which we go.

The argument about government intervention in our economic affairs dates back to our country's birth.

The most vital part of our society is our economy. If it fails, all else will fall apart. Because of this, the involvement of the government in the economy is still a point of major contention. It is an argument as old as the country itself.

The Pressing Question

1. Construct two separate definitions for the following words. The definitions are not found in the reading, but you can infer your own ideas from the topics discussed.

   a. conservative

b. liberal

B. Our Governments Today

Every time Americans get into a car and go out for fast food, they do not realize the extent to which government is involved with their lives. The car that they drive is registered with the state, manufactured according to federal standards, and will be driven on roads maintained mostly by local and state governments. The food that is bought must be supplied and prepared according to local, state, and federal cleanliness regulations. Taxes will be assessed at the time of purchase. Just on this little trip, there are a several cases where the government is involved in our lives.

The shared responsibility among local, state, and federal governments is a system called **federalism**. For example, your city maintains local parks, your state maintains your highways, and the federal government provides Social Security assistance to older people in your area. Our governments promote fairness in competition by enforcing antitrust laws, protect consumers from harmful products by inspecting food, and try to maintain economic well-being by managing social assistance programs.

Americans have come to expect quite a bit from their governments. If we are thrown out of work, we expect the government to help us out until we find another job. If there is a national emergency, the government is expected to maintain order. If there is injustice, Americans expect the government to eradicate it. These goods and services are expected by the public.

When talking about the government, it is important to note the division of products and services in our economy. They can be divided into two groups.

First, **public goods** are goods that cannot be denied to anyone. For instance, our system of national defense benefits all citizens no matter where they live or what they do. On the other hand, a **private good** is a good that can be denied to people. If you buy a new computer, it is easy to deny others the use of it. While our government protects your right to private goods (property) through the law, it is also committed to providing a myriad of public goods.

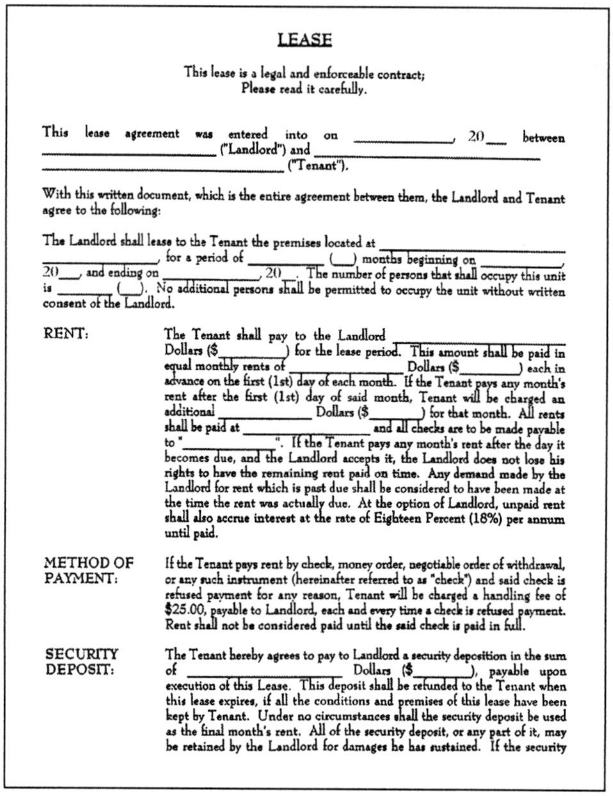

LEASE

This lease is a legal and enforceable contract;
Please read it carefully.

This lease agreement was entered into on ____________, 20___ between ______________________ ("Landlord") and ______________________ ______________________ ("Tenant").

With this written document, which is the entire agreement between them, the Landlord and Tenant agree to the following:

The Landlord shall lease to the Tenant the premises located at ______________________ ______________, for a period of ____________ (___) months beginning on ____________, 20___, and ending on ____________, 20___. The number of persons that shall occupy this unit is ________ (___). No additional persons shall be permitted to occupy the unit without written consent of the Landlord.

RENT: The Tenant shall pay to the Landlord ______________ Dollars ($__________) for the lease period. This amount shall be paid in equal monthly rents of ______________ Dollars ($__________) each in advance on the first (1st) day of each month. If the Tenant pays any month's rent after the first (1st) day of said month, Tenant will be charged an additional ______________ Dollars ($________) for that month. All rents shall be paid at ______________ and all checks are to be made payable to "______________". If the Tenant pays any month's rent after the day it becomes due, and the Landlord accepts it, the Landlord does not lose his rights to have the remaining rent paid on time. Any demand made by the Landlord for rent which is past due shall be considered to have been made at the time the rent was actually due. At the option of Landlord, unpaid rent shall also accrue interest at the rate of Eighteen Percent (18%) per annum until paid.

METHOD OF PAYMENT: If the Tenant pays rent by check, money order, negotiable order of withdrawal, or any such instrument (hereinafter referred to as "check") and said check is refused payment for any reason, Tenant will be charged a handling fee of $25.00, payable to Landlord, each and every time a check is refused payment. Rent shall not be considered paid until the said check is paid in full.

SECURITY DEPOSIT: The Tenant hereby agrees to pay to Landlord a security deposition in the sum of ______________ Dollars ($__________), payable upon execution of this Lease. This deposit shall be refunded to the Tenant when this lease expires, if all the conditions and premises of this lease have been kept by Tenant. Under no circumstances shall the security deposit be used as the final month's rent. All of the security deposit, or any part of it, may be retained by the Landlord for damages he has sustained. If the security

Contracts, like leases, are strictly enforced by our government. In order for our economy to work, a rule of law must be enforced.

One of the most important ways government protects your private property is through the enforcement of contract law. A **contract** is an agreement between two or more people to perform a service or to provide a good. This process where two parties agree to do something and cooperate is fundamental to our free-enterprise system. For instance, Mrs. Garcia signed a contract with Jones Construction to get a new bathroom. She was very specific about what she wanted and when it was to be finished. Unfortunately, when the crew left, they did not finish the job according to Mrs. Garcia's wishes and then sent her a bill for twice the contract price. Without the contract, Mrs. Garcia would be in trouble. But the local court system and government will enforce the contract and either make the company finish the job properly or allow Mrs. Garcia to sue for damages.

Throughout the twentieth century, our governments (local, state, and federal) have expanded their power to better accomplish their goals. Because our population has more than tripled (from 74 million in 1900 to over 260 million today), our government has grown to meet our growing needs. In fact, our governments are by far and away the largest employer in the country. In 1935, approximately 3.2 million people worked for local, state, and federal governments. Today, over 17 million people are public employees. Unfortunately, while our expectations for public services and goods have risen, so has the spending of our governments.

The Pressing Question

2. Elaborate on your own political opinions. Do you call yourself a liberal or conservative? Why?

C. Theories of Taxes in Our Economy

Taxes provide a cash flow so that the government can operate. This money provides for services, government regulatory agencies, and the redistribution of wealth. The amount of money that the government brings in every year in fees, charges, and taxes is known as **tax revenue**. In 1999, the U.S. government took in over 1.5 trillion dollars. Our elected representatives decide how the money is spent. How much we pay and how much we spend can have a tremendous influence on the health of our economy.

Mark Twain once remarked that there were only two sure things in life, "death and taxes." Ever since people have lived in societies, forfeiting some of their earnings or resources to the government has been an aggravation. There are many differing opinions and theories when it comes to how our government should take money from us. At the core of each opinion is the issue of fairness.

Our current federal income tax is known as a **progressive tax**. As people make more money, they will have to pay a larger percentage of their income to the government in the form of taxes. In the current system, the lowest income tax bracket is 15 percent and the highest is 39.6 percent. Many citizens argue that people who make more money should not have to pay a higher percentage. They believe that taking more of people's income will act as a **disincentive**. In other words, if individuals feel that they are paying too much in taxes, there might not be a point to make more money. They might not decide to work harder or pursue a promotion.

Opponents to progressive taxation argue for a **flat tax.** Also called a **proportional tax**, this system would take the same percentage of income from every citizen. No matter how much a person makes, each would send the same flat rate to the government. If the flat rate was 15 percent, a person who makes $1,000,000 per year would pay $150,000. A person making $10,000 would pay $1,500. Under our current tax code, the first person would pay $376,662 and the second person would pay nothing but social security tax. By doing this, the government hopes to improve the standard of living of the poor and create more financial equity in our society. Proponents of the flat-tax argue that the government is treating people who are more successful unfairly.

A **regressive tax** is a type of tax that takes a higher percentage of people's income as they make less money. State and local sales taxes are the best example of this. For example, two women go into a car dealership to buy the same $20,000 car. The sales tax on the car in county X will amount to $1,400. The first woman makes $35,000 per year. The tax amounts to 4 percent of her yearly income.

Company Name	Pay Period	Check Date	Check Number
Entire Tech Manufacturing	04/04/2001-04/17/2001	04/23/2001	10193873
Employee Name	*Social Security Number*	*Status*	*Tax Adjustments*
Jane R. Doe	000-42-0000	M-1	None

Earnings			*Taxes*			*Deductions*		
	This Pay	*Year To Date*		*This Pay*	*Year To Date*		*This Pay*	*Year To Date*
Salary	1119.00	9878.00	Federal	122.40	966.72	Annuity	100.00	1300.00
OT	158.00	442.00	State	33.12	259.87			
			FICA	69.77	555.33			
			Medicare	18.98	124.54	Charity	15.00	195.00
			City	44.33	178.17			
Bonus	57.00	695.00						
Total	1334.00	11015.00	Total	288.60	2170.76	Total	115.00	1495.00

Gross Pay	1234.00
-Taxes	288.60
-Deduction	15.00
=Net Pay	930.40

See if you can spot anything peculiar in this paycheck. Turn your attention to the Total Gross Pay in the "earnings" area. Now compare that number to the gross pay for the final paycheck amount. Why don't the numbers match up? Why do you suppose the government didn't tax that money? You'll find out in the next part about personal finance and retirement accounts.

The second woman makes $135,000 per year. The sales tax on the car will amount to about 1 percent of her income.

Opinions about fairness in taxation vary with someone's social concerns, value system, and economic position. The two basic stances are as follows:

- **Ability-to-pay principle**—Those who make more money should pay a larger portion of their income or wealth to the government. People who believe in this idea believe that the government should take an active role in procuring a more equal distribution of income in society.
- **Benefits-received principle**—This idea states that those who get more of the government services should pay for them. For example, the excise tax on gasoline is paid only by those who use gasoline. If one uses more, one pays more in taxes. While it is difficult to figure out how much a citizen benefits from other services, proponents of this theory say it is more fair because it more accurately mirrors how a free-market works. In other words, if you get a good or service from the government, you should pay for it just as you would pay any other business.

The Pressing Questions

3. Considering the differing ideas about taxation, explain what idea you consider to be most fair.

4. Based upon your stance, what political party in the United States do you believe shares your beliefs? Explain your response.

D. The Litany of Taxes

In the 1990s, the average American paid close to 40 percent of his or her income in taxes. There are numerous different destinations for one's tax dollars. Every level of our government gains operating revenue from taxes.

The largest amount of money U.S. citizens pay is to the federal government. Here are the taxes collected by our national government:

- **Income tax**—These taxes are progressive according to an individual's income. The Internal Revenue Service operates a pay-as-you-go system. By estimating your tax bill, the IRS takes a fraction from each paycheck. If they take too much money, you will get a refund. If they take too little, you will owe the difference. Every taxpayer must file the previous year's tax return (forms) by April 15. Dividends from stock and interest earned from banks are considered income. If you have ever had a job, some of the tax forms on the pay stub on the previous page should look familiar.

- **Capital Gains Tax**—If you hold an investment that has increased in value, the difference between what you sold the investment for and your purchase price is regarded a capital gain. For instance, if you buy stock that goes up in value, and you sell, you will have to pay tax on the difference. For years, money made on the sale of the house you lived in was taxed, but under the 1997 tax code, it is no longer taxable.

- **Social Security Tax**—Also known as FICA tax (Federal Insurance Cooperation Act), this money helps to support the Social Security programs that aid the elderly and the indigent. Currently, it is a flat 6.2 percent of income that is matched by employers. The rates change as incomes reach higher levels.

- **Medicare Tax—**This is a flat 1.4 percent of one's income that funds the health care of retired Americans.

- **Corporate Income Tax**—Corporations are taxed different rates according to their **net** income or profitability.

Local excise taxes and bond issues are paid for this new football stadium. Is this a good way to spend?

- **Excise Taxes**—these are taxes on particular products or services. Gasoline, tobacco, alcohol, gaming, and telephone service are just a few of the excise taxes that Americans pay.

- **Estate Taxes**—Sometimes called inheritance tax, this is imposed when a person dies and leaves money or property to another.

Our national government is not the only one to collect taxes from us. The following are some of the payments we must make to our state and local governments:

- **Sales Tax**—Most states collect sales taxes. Some counties also collect them. Thus, citizens pay a combination of sales tax to the two. In a particular state, one might pay 3 percent to the county and 4 percent to the state for a total of 7 percent.

- **Property Tax**—Homeowners and businesses pay tax on houses, buildings, and land. These taxes vary from state to state. Tax is assessed upon the estimated value of the property and then taxed according to a localities rate. For example, Lakewood, Ohio, has a rate of 2.53 percent. On a \$100,000 house, the yearly tax bill is \$2,530. This money is usually paid by homeowners when they make their monthly mortgage payment. Most communities depend on property tax to supply close to 80 percent of their operating revenue. In many parts of the country, property taxes also fund local schools.

- **Local Income Tax**—The city that you work in will deduct from your paycheck money for your estimated tax bill for the year. In Cleveland, 2 percent is taken.
- **Regional Income Tax**—In some counties, the community that you live in will also charge an income tax. If you live and work in the same city, you can avoid paying this tax.

The Pressing Question

5. If the an average American makes around $40,000 per year for his or her lifetime and works from age 22 to 65, what amount will he or she pay in taxes for their entire lifetime?

E. Develop Tax Savvy

Look to the paycheck displayed in this chapter. Notice the different taxes that are assessed. First, the largest amount will be federal withholding tax. Below that, are Social Security and Medicare taxes. The state and local income taxes are also listed. The gross pay is totaled on the lower left-hand box. After subtracting the taxes and other deductions, the remainder is known as net pay.

Knowing how to read a paycheck is vital to your financial survival. It is also handy to know a few of the basic tax forms you can expect to encounter. Some of them are as follows:

- **1040**—This is the standard federal return form. This form allows the person to account for deductions. A deduction is a certain amount of money that one can subtract from their gross yearly income. The two most common deductions are charitable contributions and interest paid on home mortgages. Separate forms must be filled in to account for these deductions.
- **1040 EZ**—This is a short version of the 1040. It is for people who don't make a lot of money and don't have any deductions to take.
- **W-2**—This is the form that your employer will send you sometime in January. It is a declaration of all the money you made and taxes you paid the previous year.
- **W-4**—This form must be filled in when you get a job. It declares how many exemptions you wish to take. Taking an **exemption** will mean that the government will take less money from each paycheck. An exemption is given for each person in a household. Remember though, if enough money is not withheld, you will pay additional tax at the time you file your return.

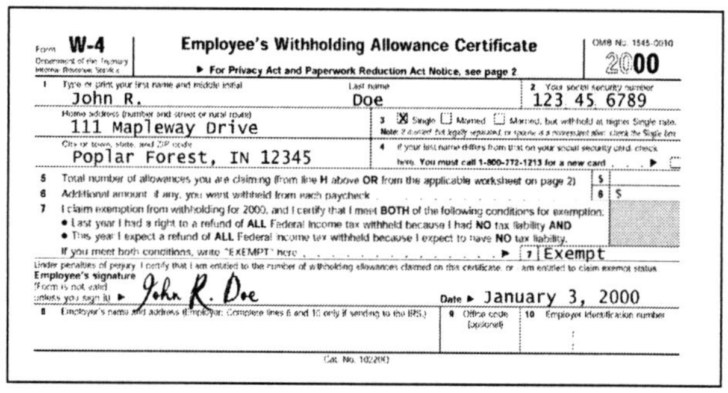
Form **W-4** — **Employee's Withholding Allowance Certificate** — OMB No. 1545-0010 — **2000**

▶ For Privacy Act and Paperwork Reduction Act Notice, see page 2.

1 Type or print your first name and middle initial: John R. — Last name: Doe — 2 Your social security number: 123 45 6789

Home address (number and street or rural route): 111 Mapleway Drive — 3 [X] Single [ ] Married [ ] Married, but withhold at higher Single rate.

City or town, state, and ZIP code: Poplar Forest, IN 12345 — 4 If your last name differs from that on your social security card, check here. You must call 1-800-772-1213 for a new card ▶ [ ]

5 Total number of allowances you are claiming (from line H above OR from the applicable worksheet on page 2) — 5

6 Additional amount, if any, you want withheld from each paycheck — 6 $

7 I claim exemption from withholding for 2000, and I certify that I meet BOTH of the following conditions for exemption:
- Last year I had a right to a refund of ALL Federal income tax withheld because I had NO tax liability AND
- This year I expect a refund of ALL Federal income tax withheld because I expect to have NO tax liability.

If you meet both conditions, write "EXEMPT" here ▶ 7 Exempt

Employee's signature (Form is not valid unless you sign it) ▶ John R. Doe — Date ▶ January 3, 2000

8 Employer's name and address (Employer: Complete lines 8 and 10 only if sending to the IRS.) — 9 Office code (optional) — 10 Employer identification number

The Pressing Question

6. How many days of the year does an average American have to work in order to pay off all of his or her taxes?

F. Basic Fiscal Policy

If people you know are described as fiscally responsible, it means that they never spend more than they make. Because of this, they avoid going into debt. Unfortunately, our national government has not been the best in its spending habits. Between 1968 and 1996, the federal government ran a yearly budget deficit. In other words, the federal government has spent more money each year than it brought in as revenue. Each time this happens, the amount of the deficit is added to our national debt. In 1997, the federal deficit was 22 billion dollars. This was added to our debt increasing it to around 5.5 trillion dollars. However, since 1998, the federal government has had a surplus.

Refer to the graphs that list where our national income comes from and where tax revenue goes to. The two largest areas of revenue for the government come from personal income and Social Security tax (about 44 percent and 38 percent respectively). Corporate tax accounts for only about 10 percent of our tax revenue. On the other end of the process, our national budget funds many programs. The four largest include national defense, social security, welfare programs, and Medicare. Four programs (Social Security, Medicare, welfare, and Medicaid) add up to over 60 percent of all Congress' spending in a year. Congress has to maintain these programs according to the laws that started them. These mandatory expenditures are often called **entitlements**. Not to be forgotten is the interest that lenders expect us to pay on our debt. We spend close to 15 percent of the yearly budget on paying the interest (not the principal) of our national debt. Over two-hundred billion dollars a year goes to bondholders, local financial institutions, and foreign banks. Just think what that $200 billion could have bought!

Thinking like an economist is important when discussing the federal budget. For instance, if part of the budget is spent on education benefits for college students, that means that the money will not be spent somewhere else, such as national defense or national parks. Remember that even the government has **opportunity costs**. This is why the arguments in the halls of Congress are so passionate. Nobody wants to sacrifice the programs that benefit their constituents.

The budget process starts with the president. He will propose a plan with the help of the General Accounting Office (which does the research of figures) and submit it to Congress early in the year. In his proposal, he and his advisors will estimate the next year's tax revenue and then suggest how that money should be allocated to different programs. For instance, in 1993, President Bill Clinton proposed cuts to defense in order to increase spending on social programs. Once Congress has the budget, they will discuss it in subcommittees. With the help of the **Congressional Budget Office** (CBO), representatives and senators will verify the president's calculations and estimates. Many congressmen will propose their own budgets. They spend much time trying to compromise between everybody's wants and wishes.

Where the Federal Government Gets Its Money, 2000

A Revenue of 1,815 Billion (projected)

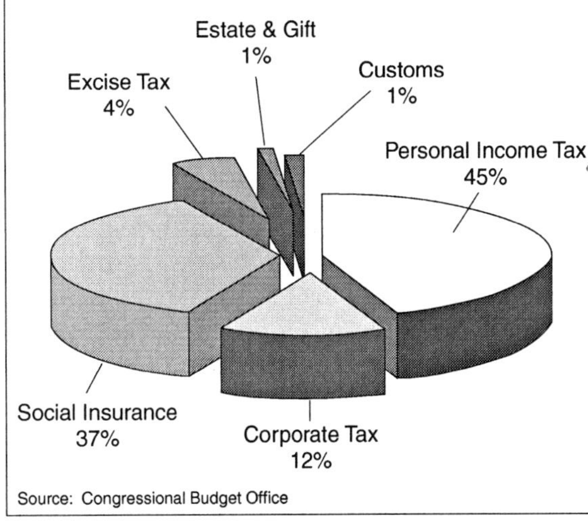

Source: Congressional Budget Office

In the **Joint Conference Committee**, members of the House and Senate try to reach a consensus. If one is met, the budget will be voted upon on the floor of first the House and then the Senate. If it passes both houses of

Congress, the proposal will go to the desk of the president. He then has the option of signing it into law, or he can **veto** it for a variety of reasons. Because the government's fiscal year runs from October 1 to September 30, the budget debates must start early in the year. If a budget is not agreed upon by the end of September, the government will usually operate on the previous year's budget. However, in 1994 and 1995, Congress refused to continue on the old budget and held back funds from government agencies resulting in several government shutdowns.

Where Our Tax Dollars Go, 2000

Total Budget of $1,684 Billion (projected)

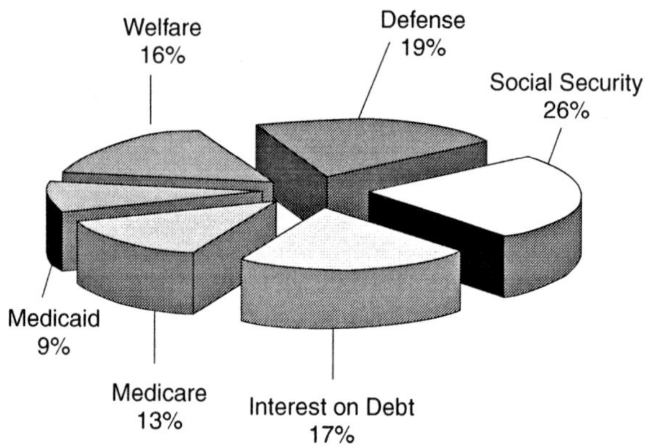

Source: Congressional Budget Office

In 1996, the president and Congress reached an impasse. Neither was willing to compromise on a budget, so Congress refused to continue to fund federal programs. For several weeks, only the most basic services were being provided for. Many federal employees were sent home, and national parks were shut down. It demonstrated to the public that compromise is essential in fiscal policy. While Congress ultimately holds the purse strings, the power is distributed over three branches of our government.

Before the early 1900s, there was no federal income tax in our country. The federal government wielded little fiscal power. The federal income tax, however, changed all that. In the 1930s, Franklin Delano Roosevelt started a great deal of new government programs. His New Deal created new expectations from the public. People now expect the government to perform many tasks in society from paving roads to caring for the elderly. More programs started during Lyndon Johnson's Great Society furthered the reach of the federal government. Welfare, Medicare, and food stamps, which were unthinkable in the past, became part of our normal operation.

However, there was a change of course in the latter-half of the 1990s. Because of the good economy, more people are working. This means that they will be paying more taxes. Increased tax revenue has helped Congress balance the budget. In fact, in 1998, there was a $70 billion surplus—the first one since 1968. Nobody had anticipated that. Now the politicians are bickering about how the extra money should be spent. The extra money is actually a windfall of extra income and Social Security tax collected due to the booming economy.

It is important that the government not run too large a deficit. If it uses too much of our limited resources, interest rates could be driven higher, pushing some consumers out of the marketplace. This is called **crowding out.**

The Pressing Question

7. If we have a budget surplus in the years to come, how should the money be spent?

G. Theories on Fiscal Policy

While Democrats and Republicans argue about their different agendas on federal programs, their policies are divided between liberal and conservative ideas. Economists have long argued about what role the government should play in the economy. How much should we be taxed? How much should the government spend on social programs? The two main views on how these questions are answered are divided into supply-side and demand-side economics.

Supply-Side Theory originated in the 1700s with a French economist named Jean-Baptiste Say. The theory holds the premise that most government intervention is harmful to a nation's economy. Excessive rules and regulations in combination with high taxation will stifle the growth of business. In the end, slow business activity will cost jobs. The theory is aimed at promoting growth by providing incentives to producers to produce more. Say is best known for **Say's Law**, which states that "supply creates its own demand." This idea states that if firms produce more goods and services, inflation will be reduced as more goods are created to fill the demand.

A modern champion of supply-side economics was Ronald Reagan. Right after he took office in 1981, the former governor of California proposed his budget. It called for tax cuts on individuals, spending cuts on social programs, and regulatory reform. Reagan used the ideas of an economist named Arthur Laffer. The Laffer curve (as shown below) states that too much taxation will be a disincentive to work. But, if taxes are lowered, people will work harder, and the result will be higher government revenue. Opponents of Reaganomics argued that the tax breaks to business and the rich were unnecessary and harmful. Because of this, Reagan's fiscal reforms were known as "trickle-down economics." The tax breaks and regulatory reform were to bring more prosperity to business and those benefits would trickle down to the lower classes of society.

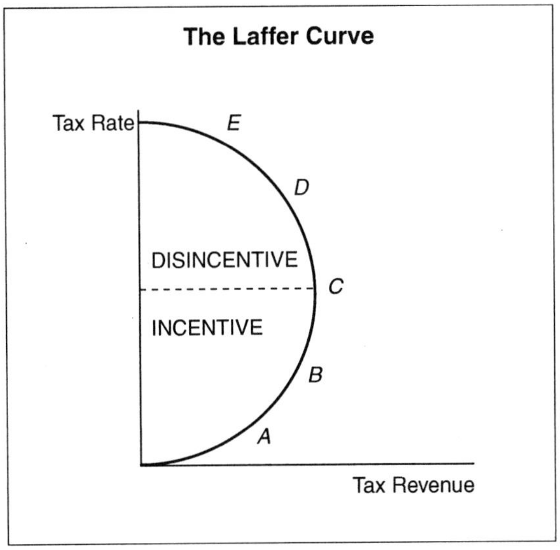

Demand-Side Theory originated in the 1930s with the writings John Maynard Keynes (rhymes with rains). In the book *The General Theory of Employment, Interest, and Money*, Keynes stated that the government can stabilize the economy by controlling the aggregate demand of a nation's citizens. He also stated that one could calculate aggregate demand by using a formula for GDP (refer to Part 3). A government can lower taxes and start social programs when the economy is bad. If inflation is threatening, taxes can be raised and programs slashed. While this might require deficit-spending, it may cause consumers and businesses to buy less, and inflation may subside. Keynes hoped that government intervention would eliminate the boom and bust trends of the 1800s and prevent damaging depressions in the future.

Today, involvement in the economy by our national government can be divided into two categories:

- **Discretionary Spending**—These are policies that Congress can change in response to fluctuations in the economy. Among these actions are changes in tax rates and changes in spending on a variety of programs.
- **Nondiscretionary Spending**—These are also known as **automatic stabilizers**. In other words, these measures will kick in to affect the economy whether or not Congress acts. For instance, in a bad economy, our progressive tax system will aid those whose income drops, because they will drop in tax brackets. Overall tax receipts automatically fall, leaving more money in the hands of consumers. If they spend this, the GDP should increase. Also, programs like welfare and unemployment compensation will automatically aid those who qualify for it. In essence, the programs use tax dollars to benefit citizens who are included. These **transfer payments** are another chief stabilizer of the economy.

The Pressing Question

8. Consider the arguments for supply-side and demand-side economics. List three reasons why you believe more strongly in one or the other.

H. Controlling the Economy

Strategies of both supply-side and demand-side theories can be divided into two basic groups. Just like the Fed, Congress has various ways to control the economy.

- **Expansionary Policy**—When the economy slumps, the government can lower taxes, reduce regulation on business, and increase spending. Because of the slow economy, tax revenue will be down. Keynes argued that the government should incur a deficit temporarily.
- **Contractionary Policy**—If inflation becomes too high, it could seriously damage the economy. The government can act by lowering spending on social programs and raising taxes. The higher taxes would take the money out of the hands of business and consumers and the lack of social spending would slow down spending as well.

Demand-siders and supply-siders may advocate a combination of the ideas above. People who are more conservative tend to believe that the economy should stabilize itself through the actions of the market. Demand-siders are the ones who want the full government involvement.

United States Federal Budget, 1970–2003

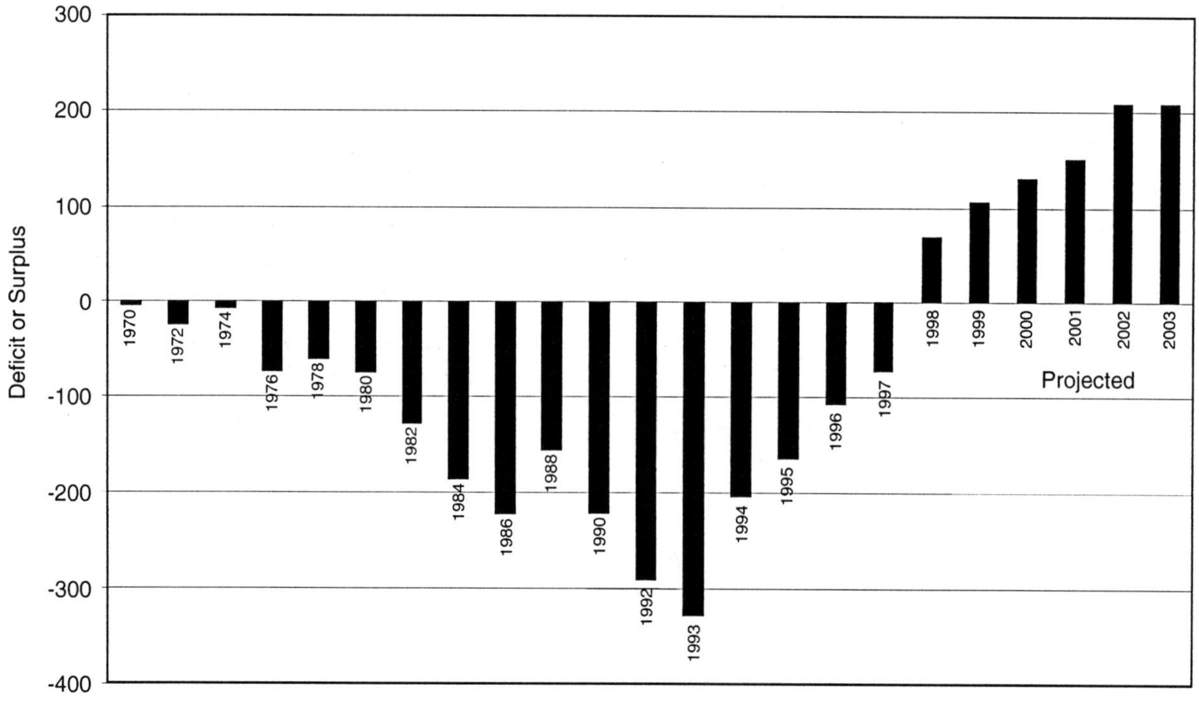

Source: Congressional Budget Office

The Pressing Question

9. Use your knowledge of conservative and liberal viewpoints to associate the two with supply-side or demand-side theory. Which goes with which and why?

I. The Multiplier Effect

One major consideration that both supply and demand-siders need to consider is what will happen when they choose to cut the tax rate. People will spend a certain amount of extra money that they get. This is known as the **marginal propensity to consume** (MPC). However, they will also save a fraction of it as well. This is known as the **marginal propensity to save** (MPS). In the United States, our citizens will tend to have a lower MPS than people from other countries.

In general though, how much people spend or save depends on how the economy is doing. When the economy is doing well, people feel better about their futures and thus will tend to spend more money. On the other hand, if times are tough, extra money will be closely guarded and saved. Therefore, a tax cut might not have as much effect in a period of recession.

The **multiplier effect** occurs when a small change in someone's income will ripple throughout the economy, resulting in larger changes in spending. For instance, if Congress cuts taxes by $100 billion, and the marginal propensity to save is .10, the people will spend $90 billion. This means that the 90 billion will end up back in the pockets of consumers. Those consumers will save 10 percent ($9 billion), and spend the rest ($81 billion). This trend continues until one trillion dollars have been added to the economy. But, if the MPC is lower, say at 0.5, the overall impact of the tax cut will be much lower.

The Pressing Question

10. Fill in the following chart with the necessary information.

MPC	MPC
.89	______
______	.17
.72	______

J. Our Government Regulates

A **regulation** is a law or legally binding ruling passed by local, state, or federal government that business must follow. To enforce these laws and to guard against violations, our governments have numerous agencies to watch businesses. Here are just a few of the more prominent regulatory agencies:

- **Securities and Exchange Commission**—Watches for insider trading and fraudulent activity in the bond, stock, and future markets.
- **Federal Deposit Insurance Corporation**—Insures bank deposits up to $100,000.
- **Federal Communications Commission**—Issues the licenses for the use of public airwaves.
- **Occupational Safety and Health Administration**—Inspects workplaces and sets standards for job safety.
- **Federal Trade Commission**—Watches for infractions of U.S. antitrust law.

Even our representatives in city hall strive to keep their constituents happy.

- **Food and Drug Administration**—Inspects the nation's food supply along with the Department of Agriculture. This agency is also in charge of approving new drugs for the marketplace.
- **Consumer Product Safety Commission**—Inspects and tests the safety of new products.
- **Environmental Protection Agency**—Sets standards for industry and oversees the inspection of the fitness of the environment.

Opponents of regulation say that too many rules and laws cost too much money for businesses to follow and hurt productivity in the end. Others argue that businesses would abuse consumers, workers, and the environment if it were not for the government acting as the watchdog. Like all issues in economics, regulations have two sides to consider. While a rule or law is intended to do one thing, there will always be an opportunity cost to weigh.

The Pressing Question

11. How much regulation should the government impose upon business? Are they too involved or not involved enough?

K. Campaign Finance and Pork

In recent years, and most especially in congressional and presidential elections, the role of fundraising has become a more distressing issue. In 1996, the Dole and Clinton campaigns spent a combined $800 million. To raise the kind of capital it takes to run the modern campaign of television and printed advertising, candidates must start fundraising almost as soon as the last election is over.

Under current law, an individual is limited to giving $1,000 to a single candidate. However, there are no limits on how much money may be given to a political party. In this way, a contributor may give as much as he or she wishes to a party and then earmark it for a specific candidate. In return for this **soft money** and other contributions, politicians will offer assistance in passing favorable legislation for the contributor.

Many businesses and special interest groups pool their money together into what is known as a **political action committee**. In these organizations, resources are pooled, and because there is no limit to the donation size of a PAC, as they are known, a considerable amount of cash can be channeled to a candidate. These larger contributions should, in theory, garner greater influence on the decisions a legislator or executive makes.

To keep constant pressure on our elected representatives, many PACs hire **lobbyists** to roam the halls of Congress to put direct pressure on the members of Congress to make favorable decisions. For instance, if there is a pending vote in Congress to decide on requiring

Government projects demonstrate the enormous capital resources available to all levels of government. Things like new stadiums are but one involvement of our governments.

American car makers to lower the emissions of their vehicles, several environmental lobbies will dispatch lobbyists to Congress to remind certain representatives of their responsibility to the environment and to their organization. On the other hand, the automakers will also have lobbyists of their own trying to exact some influence on the congressional vote.

The concern is that representatives at national, state, and local levels are more loyal to their contributors than they are to their **constituents** or to their own political beliefs. Ideally, we elect people to represent us and to make decisions that will improve our lives, protect us from harm, and see that our liberties are kept in tact. However, many fear that a system so dependent upon money will cloud the true nature of our **representative democracy**. Are your representatives keeping your best interests in mind? Or are they voting to keep the big money contributors happy? Do you know your representatives' voting records?

In 1997, Congress convened a **bipartisan** (two party) commission to look into the methods of donation collection used by both parties during the 1996 elections. This committee, led by Ohio Democrat Senator John Glenn and Tennessee Republican Senator Fred Thompson, has exposed the vast amounts of money raised by the 1996 campaigns. Not only has the amount of money become evident, but also the fact that many contributions were coming from foreign companies and other noncitizens of the United States has raised the issue of **campaign finance reform** to public scrutiny. Some citizens worry that representatives will not govern in the best interest of their constituents. In the past, loopholes have always been found to skirt laws and get money to the candidates. In this recent attempt to reform the system, Congress' ability to make money less of an issue in our political system remains to be seen.

Another lasting given in national government is something called **pork-barrel politics.** In order to be reelected, a member of Congress must not only raise the money to campaign, but also get the votes. To ensure this, senators and representatives will seek funds for special projects that will bring jobs and money to the home district or state. If people benefit, they will feel good about the job Congress is doing and vote for the **incumbent**. Members of Congress have a way of helping one another do this. If one senator needs a bill passed to fund a "pork" project, he or she might ask another senator to vote for it in exchange for a future vote or favor. This practice of **logrolling** sometimes forces a representative to vote for a bill not out of conscience or belief, but to return a favor from the past.

Our elected officials seem to like their jobs. They campaign fiercely and raise huge amounts of money to keep them. While in office, they will often strike deals for pork projects that cost the taxpayers millions of dollars just to maintain their popularity. Some people say that our democracy is deteriorating under the strain. Others maintain it is just a continuation of the past and it is all business as usual.

However you look at it, our government is big, wasteful, and even a bit intrusive. In the two hundred years since the writing of the Constitution, it has managed to change with the times, survive a civil war, overcome depressions, and build a monstrous debt. For better or for worse, it is still around, and it is the system that you have inherited!

The Pressing Question

12. When a candidate receives large sums of money from a corporation or PAC, many people consider this a **conflict of interest**. What do you suppose they mean by that?

Name________________________

Date________________________

Reading and Vocabulary

Directions: For each of the blanks in the following story, choose a boldfaced word in your reading that best completes the sentence.

January 18, 1998 (1) ___________ thinkers, critical of congressional Democrats' new budget proposals, have asked for a (2) ___________ commission to settle disputes over spending issues. The issue arose when liberals in both the Senate and the House discovered that for the first time since 1968, the federal government would not run a deficit but would have a (3) ___________. Republicans have been arguing for weeks that any extra tax (4) ___________ should be used to pay down the $5.5 trillion (5) ___________ . Some more vociferous cries from the right argued for reform of our tax system stating that a (6) ___________ tax is inherently unfair because it penalizes those people who make more money. The Democrats, on the other hand, would like to see big (7) ___________ programs like Social Security and Medicare bolstered for the future.

The old mantra of (8) ___________-side economics made itself known again in Washington as special interest groups and their (9) ___________ worked the halls of Congress seeking lower regulation and lower taxes on corporations. This flies in the face of the Keynsian (10) ___________-siders' belief that taxing and spending with occasional deficit spending can be an effective means of controlling an economy. They propose that surpluses in the future be channeled into (11) ___________ spending programs like student loans. They seemed to be bowing to pressure from (12) ___________ action committees that represent children and college students. When a rider which would send money to Ohio to build a $35 million addition to the University of Akron's Primate Research Lab was added to the bill, representatives from the GOP cried foul claiming that the idea was merely a brash form of (13) ___________ politics.

States are also hoping to benefit from the windfall at the federal level. A board of governors meeting in Atlanta proclaimed that the spirit of shared power and (14) ___________ dictated that the national government should necessitate a reevaluation of the appropriation of excess funds. Officials from the Congressional (15) ___________ Office, however, claimed that (16) ___________ payments like those in Social Security fell under the heading of (17) ___________ spending and could not be touched by any redirecting of funds. As one unnamed source claimed, "As soon as the money was discovered, the states immediately demanded their share." The person continued, "People just received their (18) ______________ forms and have just started doing their taxes . . . for heaven's sake, (19) ___________ 15 is a long way off and the states are already beating down our doors." In any case, it seems our days of (20) ___________ spending and a rapidly accumulating debt are over. Let's see if Washington can mess that one up! Most everyone asked for his or her opinion declined to comment.

Name____________________

Date____________________

Doing Your Taxes

Directions: Using the information given to you in class, fill out this tax form to find out whether you get a refund or a bill!

Department of the Treasury—Internal Revenue Service

Form **1040EZ** **Income Tax Return for Single and Joint Filers With No Dependents** (99) **1999** OMB No. 1545-0675

Use the IRS label here

Your first name and initial | Last name

If a joint return, spouse's first name and initial | Last name

Home address (number and street). If you have a P.O. box, see page 12. | Apt. no.

City, town or post office, state, and ZIP code. If you have a foreign address, see page 12.

Your social security number

Spouse's social security number

▲ IMPORTANT! ▲ You **must** enter your SSN(s) above.

Presidential Election Campaign (See page 12.)

Note. *Checking "Yes" will not change your tax or reduce your refund.*

Do you want $3 to go to this fund? ▶ Yes ☐ No ☐

If a joint return, does your spouse want $3 to go to this fund? ▶ Yes ☐ No ☐

Dollars **Cents**

Income

Attach Copy B of Form(s) W-2 here. Enclose, but do not staple, any payment.

1 Total wages, salaries, and tips. This should be shown in box 1 of your W-2 form(s). Attach your W-2 form(s). 1

2 Taxable interest. If the total is over $400, you cannot use Form 1040EZ. 2

3 Unemployment compensation, qualified state tuition program earnings, and Alaska Permanent Fund dividends (see page 14). 3

4 Add lines 1, 2, and 3. This is your **adjusted gross income.** 4

Note. You **must** check Yes or No.

5 Can your parents (or someone else) claim you on their return?
Yes. Enter amount from worksheet on back. ☐
No. If **single**, enter 7,050.00. If **married**, enter 12,700.00. See back for explanation. ☐ 5

6 Subtract line 5 from line 4. If line 5 is larger than line 4, enter 0. This is your **taxable income.** ▶ 6

Payments and tax

7 Enter your Federal income tax withheld from box 2 of your W-2 form(s). 7

8a **Earned income credit** (see page 15).
b Nontaxable earned income: enter type and amount below.
Type | $ 8a

9 Add lines 7 and 8a. These are your **total payments.** 9

10 **Tax.** Use the amount on **line 6 above** to find your tax in the tax table on pages 24–28 of the booklet. Then, enter the tax from the table on this line. 10

Refund

Have it directly deposited! See page 20 and fill in 11b, 11c, and 11d.

11a If line 9 is larger than line 10, subtract line 10 from line 9. This is your **refund.** 11a

▶ b Routing number

▶ c Type: Checking ☐ Savings ☐

d Account number

Amount you owe

12 If line 10 is larger than line 9, subtract line 9 from line 10. This is the **amount you owe.** See page 21 for details on how to pay. 12

I have read this return. Under penalties of perjury, I declare that to the best of my knowledge and belief, the return is true, correct, and accurately lists all amounts and sources of income I received during the tax year.

Sign here ▶ Keep copy for your records.

Your signature | Spouse's signature if joint return. See page 11.

Date | Your occupation | Date | Spouse's occupation

For Official Use Only 1 2 3 4 5 6 7 8 9 10

For Disclosure, Privacy Act, and Paperwork Reduction Act Notice, see page 23. Cat. No. 11329W 1999 Form 1040EZ

Name________________________

Date________________________

Problems and Solutions

Directions: Your group is to read the following problems together. Your task is to do the following:

1. Locate and determine the main problem.
2. Propose one multifaceted solution.
3. Determine a plan of action to get that solution implemented.
4. Address the opposition you expect would rise against you.

You will be graded on the final product and your performance during the class.

1. Schooling in this country is primarily left up to the discretion of the states and not the federal government. However, schools are funded mostly by the money collected from local property tax. This translates into better schools for wealthier areas and inadequate schools in less fortunate districts. Is it fair that someone who is from a poor neighborhood had $3,500 a year spent on them and another had $12,000? This is the current situation in many states. Is it in violation of any laws that you know of? How can you go about changing the situation if you wanted to? Propose a solution.

2. Both major party candidates for president in 1996 spent a combined $800,000,000. The average candidate for the senate spent about $25 million per race. Special interests that represent everything from tobacco to the elderly funnel money to many different candidates in order to have their wishes considered in congress. There is a cap of $1,000 a person can contribute to a candidate, and $5,000 that one can give to a party. However, there are loopholes that allow people to donate any amount (soft money) they wish to PACs and other special interest groups. How do we reform campaign finance if it must start with congress? What proposal do you offer to solve the problem and how can you influence congress into passing it? (Keep in mind that recently the Supreme Court has declared that campaign contributions are a form of free speech protected by the First Amendment!)

3. Demographically, the United States is getting much older. The baby boomers are all between the ages of 40 and 55 and account for about 25 percent of the population. Not only that, but our life expectancy is increasing every year, meaning that these "boomers" will be retired for a long long time. This is not yet a problem for Social Security. There are more people working in the United States than are retired. We tax people 7 percent of their income, which is matched by their employers, and that has been enough to ensure a surplus of money and the viability of the system in the short term. However, by 2010, there will be a shortage of funds as more people retire at age 65 and start collecting benefits. How will we sustain the current $360 billion dollar program when the cost of it will possibly triple in the future? Can we deny benefits to people who have been paying into a system for their entire working lives? Can we afford to discontinue the program and let old people suffer? What will you have when you retire? Propose a solution.

4. When President Johnson started Medicare in 1967, it was to stop old people from having to make decisions between health care and to other essentials that they need to live. It has grown into a $280 billion program. We pay for it with a 3.5 percent tax on each worker in the United States. With inflation at 3 percent, Medicare has been growing at a rate of almost 12 percent a year. Benefits have not increased, but costs certainly have. Much of the money has been spent on fraudulent claims. People unlawfully get someone's Medicare number and then charge the government for bogus items. It is estimated that almost 20 percent of what Medicare spends is actually on fraud. Must we cut the system? How can Medicare save money and cut fraud? Will it be able to survive when a majority of this country is retired? Propose a solution.

Name________________________

Date________________________

The Layers of Government

Directions: With the help of your group, find the following information, and place it in the space provided.

1. National Source ____________________
   a. President____________________
   b. Vice President ____________________
   c. Current Federal Tax Revenue ____________________
   d. Secretary of Treasury____________________
   e. Secretary of Labor ____________________
   f. Chair of the Federal Reserve ____________________
   g. Secretary of State ____________________
   h. Attorney General____________________
   i. Your Congressional District ____________________
   j. Top and Bottom Tax Brackets____________________

2. State Source ____________________
   a. Governor ____________________
   b. Lieutenant Governor ____________________
   c. Your State Senator ____________________
   d. Your State Representative ____________________
   e. Number of Electoral Votes____________________
   f. Sources of Revenue____________________
   g. Current Tax Revenue ____________________

3. County Source ____________________
   a. County Commissioners ____________________
   b. County Auditors ____________________
   c. Sources of Tax Revenue ____________________
   d. Current Tax Revenue ____________________
   e. Number of Employees ____________________

4. Local Source ____________________
   a. Mayor ____________________
   b. Form of Legislature____________________
   c. City Representative ____________________
   d. Your City District____________________
   e. Population ____________________
   f. Tax Revenue ____________________
   g. Last Levy Effort ____________________

Name____________________________

Date____________________________

Political Cartoons

Directions: Provide a description of what is happening in each of the following political cartoons. Then explain what the viewpoint of the cartoonist is and what he or she is trying to say.

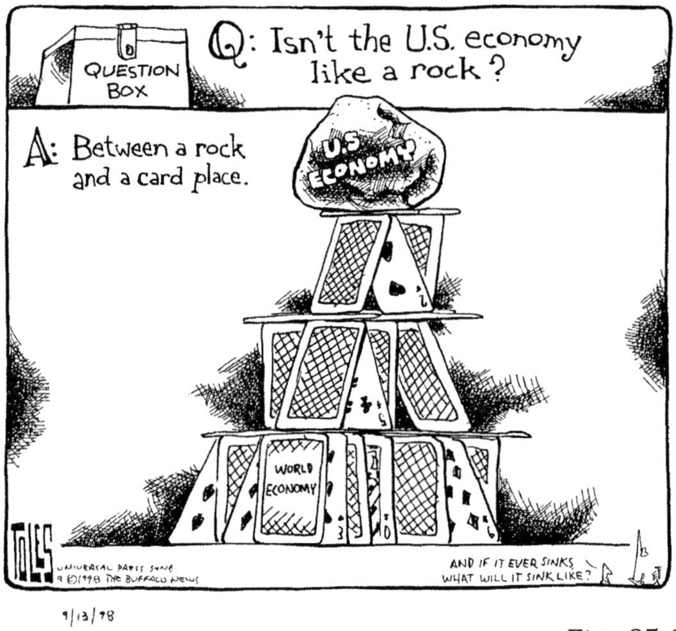

Fig. 25.1.

Fig. 25.2.

Name_________________________

Date__________________________

My Government Research

Part A.

Directions: Using your school's resources, local library system, or the Internet, research one of the following topics. Be prepared to present your findings in class.

1. SEC
2. FDIC
3. NRA
4. FCC
5. CPSC
6. CBO
7. AARP
8. OSHA
9. FDA
10. EPA

a. Name of Topic

b. Year Founded

c. Involvement in the Economy

d. Yearly Budget

e. Five Recent Headlines

Name________________________

Date________________________

Part B.

Directions: Answer the following questions.

1. Does the government have too much regulatory power over business in the United States?

2. Which governments are in charge of regulating businesses in your area?

3. Why is it important to study and understand lobbies like the NRA?

4. How do regulatory agencies get businesses to behave and follow the law?

Name____________________

Date____________________

Take a Stand?

Directions: Summarize the parties' platforms by stating where they stand on the following issues.

Part A.

Democrats	Issues	Republicans
	Environment	
	Labor	
	Taxes	
	Regulation	
	Supply-side theory	
	Demand-side theory	
	Federalism	
	Defense	
	Campaign finance	
	Welfare	
	Social Security	
	Medicare	
	Budget surpluses	
	Hamilton or Jefferson	
	Gun control	

Name__________________________

Date___________________________

Part B.

Directions: Write a three- to five-paragraph essay in which you state your own personal political beliefs. Be prepared to present your essay in class.

Part 5
Personal Finance

Questions to Consider

1. How much money does it take to retire comfortably?
2. What sort of career will provide the lifestyle that I wish to lead later in life?
3. Where is the best place to save money?
4. How does interest work?
5. Why do I pay so much for car insurance?
6. How much does the average house cost per month?
7. How much will it cost me to buy a car in the future?
8. What is credit?
9. Is it a good idea to use credit cards?
10. How do I invest in the stock market?

Terms You Need in Order to Read

Investment	Bonds	Yield
Interest	Market	Money
Stock		

Name________________________

Date________________________

Personal Finance

Directions: Read the selection, and answer the Pressing Questions as you read. Be prepared for class discussion.

A. Career Goals

In the near future, you will be coming to a crossroads in your life. Upon graduating from high school, you will have to decide whether you should immediately pursue a career or go to college. Even tougher than this will be your eventual choice of career. The work that we do, as much as anything else, defines and molds who we are. Too many young people take this decision lightly and think that they have plenty of time to make a choice. Before they know it, they have been doing a job for five or ten years and come to the conclusion that they do not like what they do.

Note the charts below and on the next page that indicate how certain education levels dictate average salaries in the United States. In the past, it was possible for someone with only a high school education to advance to the upper levels of a corporation. However, in today's job market, businesses are usually unwilling to promote beyond a certain level if an employee does not have a college degree. While many high school graduates can secure work for a while, they will often have to go back to school to attain a degree or advanced skill.

Another factor that makes education beyond high school vital to your work is the

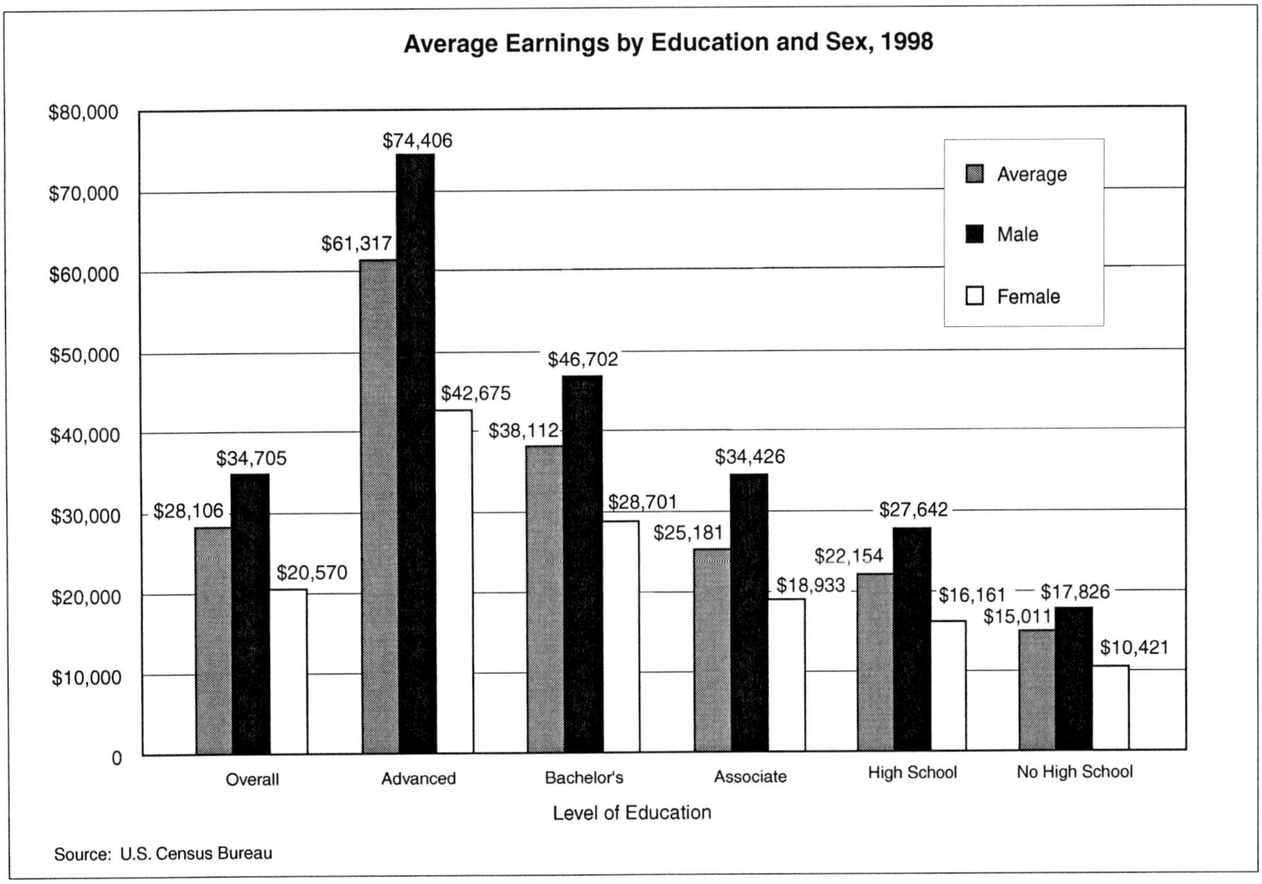

changing nature of careers today. **Job security**, or the duration that a worker can expect to have a job, does not exist like it did in past decades. Many companies have made **downsizing**, or the elimination of jobs, a common occurrence. While a high school graduate in the 1950s could find a lifetime job, buy a house, and raise a family, workers today rarely plan to work their entire life for one company. In fact, even people with college degrees will, on average, switch jobs from five to eight times in their lives. Being out of work is scary. A college degree or higher skill training will make it easier to switch jobs if it becomes necessary. Regardless, the only sure thing in today's economy is uncertainty.

As discussed in the second part, a worker's skill level will determine the demand for his labor. If someone goes to college and attains a specialized skill, he or she will be in high demand; thus, the person can expect a high salary. You need to decide what type of lifestyle you wish to live after college. If you want comfort or job security, a college degree is a necessity now more than ever.

Fastest Growing Career Avenues, 1999

Degree	Increase in Growth
Database Administration	+118%
Computer Engineer	+109%
Systems Analyst	+103%
Personal Home Care	+88%
Physical Therapy	+78%
Medical Assisting	+75%
Desktop Publishing	+72%

Source: U.S. Department of the Census

Lastly, it is never too soon to start thinking seriously about a career. Ask yourself what class you enjoy the most. It may be the class that you find the easiest, or it could be a subject that comes quickly to you. If you do not enjoy any of your classes, perhaps there is an extracurricular or hobby about which you are passionate. If you are interested in anything, there is probably a career that will suit your interests. Again, choose work that you enjoy. There are few things more depressing than being stuck in a job you find unfulfilling.

The Pressing Questions

1. Name three hobbies or classes you enjoy.

2. Name three careers that you think would correspond to the items you listed above.

B. Budget Your Money

Sooner than you think, you will come face to face with the job market. Your education may well dictate your starting salary. Note some of the various careers listed on the chart to the left. While these are national averages between 1998 and 1999, they can give you a basic idea of what to expect.

Steve recently graduated from college. He just got a job in sales with a local heating and cooling company. His base salary will be $17,500 with a possibility of $3,000 in bonuses and incentives. Steve expects to make $19,000 for his first year of work out of college. It may sound like a paltry sum, but some starting salaries in business are under $20,000 per year.

Steve has decided not to live at home but go out on his own. He is confident of his ability to succeed and survive in the "real world." On his mother's advice, he has decided to work out a monthly budget. At $19,000, Steve can expect a gross monthly income of about $1,584. He will get paid on the fifteenth and thirtieth of every month, and there will be a new assortment of bills he will expect to see.

By not living at home, there are considerable **opportunity costs** that must be dealt with. Keep in mind for every dollar spent, the money is not going somewhere else. Some of the bigger categories of expenses Steve will have to deal with are as follows:

- **Housing**—This should cost somewhere between 25 to 35 percent of your gross monthly salary. Steve found a one-bedroom apartment for $450. Housing is usually a top expense.
- **Automobile**—Steve chose a modest, mid-size car which will cost him $220 per month for the next five years. He maintains that public transportation was not an option for someone in sales.
- **Auto Insurance**—Because Steve is a male under the age of 25, he is in the highest risk group. For moderate coverage, Steve will pay $110 per month.
- **Utilities**—These include gas, electric, water, cable, and phone bills. Steve expects to pay around $150 per month for all of them.
- **Student Loans**—Steve borrowed money to finish the last two years of his education. He has a student loan of $24,000 to pay off. It will cost him $150 per month for the next fifteen years.
- **Food**—Steve is used to living like a Spartan from his experience in college. He maintains he will eat for less than $200 per month.
- **Savings**—Steve is really smart. He will save as much as possible for a down payment on a house and for his own retirement. He has decided on an automatic withdrawal from his paychecks of $150 per month.

While just covering the basics, Steve will have outlays of roughly $1,080 per month. Remember that his **gross monthly income** will be $1,584. Do not forget that he still has to pay taxes. He can expect to lose 30 percent of his salary right off the top.

In the end, Steve has $1,108 net monthly income while his expenses are only $28 less than that. Steve has some difficult decisions to make. He will definitely need more than $28 per month in spending money. At this point, he has no furniture, no computer, no gas in his car, an old stereo, and a pathetic CD collection. Living at home does not look as bad as it used to!

The Pressing Questions

3. What is the opportunity cost of Steve not living at home?

4. What would you suggest he do with the money if he were to move back in with the folks?

5. Are there any other options for Steve other than moving home? How can he afford to live on his own?

C. Managing Your Cash Flow

It is important that you keep track of exactly where your money is going. The easiest way to do that is through a checking account. These accounts are extremely **liquid** and allow the depositor to draw checks on the balance. Checks are widely accepted in a variety of transactions. Without them, people would need to carry large amounts of cash. Furthermore, it would be very risky to pay bills by mail with cash. Checking accounts make financial transactions easier.

An account can be opened simply by visiting your local bank and making a minimum deposit. The bank will then issue checks in your name. When you write a check to someone, that person will then take it to his or her bank and deposit it into his or her own account. The check will travel to the local Federal Reserve branch or other agency to be cleared. The clearing process is when an institution verifies that your account has the proper funds. If you do, money will be transferred electronically between the two banks in question and the check will be sent to your bank. At the end of the month, your bank will send the cleared check to you. If you do not have sufficient funds in your account, the check will be sent back to the recipient's bank. This is known as **"bouncing"** a check. This will end up costing the writer anywhere from $25 to $75 in penalty fees.

In the small check on this page, notice the various features of a check. All checks will have the name of the issuer and the name of the bank printed on the front. Along the bottom will be the numerical code of the bank. The second set of the numbers will be the number of the account that the money will come from. When writing a check, one should include the date, name of the recipient, the amount in numbers, the amount in words, and the writer's signature. Checking accounts come with a convenient registry in which the account holder can keep track of the balance.

When balancing a checking account, cleared checks are compared to the entries in the registry. A **debit** is registered any time money is taken from an account. A **credit** is any deposit or addition made to an account. Checks are catalogued by number, date, and description. At the end of the month, it is wise to make sure that checks written have cleared. This will help the account holder calculate an accurate **balance**, or money left in the account.

Checking accounts have recently become more difficult to manage as conveniences increase. The major innovation in banking has been the ATM (Automatic Teller Machine). These machines offer customers constant access to account information and cash. Even more recently, banks and credit card agencies have collaborated to develop ATM cards with credit card logos on them. These **debit cards** allow the holder to buy with money from a checking account anywhere a credit card is accepted. While this is a very convenient service, it is important to keep track of receipts because it is very easy to bounce a check when an accurate balance is not kept.

Tom Phillips 2298
2298 Nonaker Drive
Weehawken, NJ 12345

Date *July 2, 2000*

Pay to the order of *Pizza Express* $*15.25*

Fifteen and 25/100 dollars

HOME OFFICE BANK

For ____________ *Tom Phillips*

000-123-456789 **012 3456 78910**

The Pressing Question

6. How does one end up bouncing a check?

Banks are now appearing in places you would not expect. This is a trend in banking where mergers and downsizing echo a increasingly competitive marketplace.

D. Saving Money in the Short Term

In part 3, the topic of banks was addressed. Banks make money by taking in deposits and then lending the money to other people at a higher interest rate. But because checking and savings accounts can be **liquidated**, or changed into cash at any time, they will never pay high **yields** (or returns on your money). The more time you promise the bank that you will let them use the money, the higher the interest rate the bank will generally offer.

People save money for several reasons. They may be saving for a big purchase such as a car or a house. They might save for a child's college education or for their own retirement. Saving money wisely can bring a certain amount of financial freedom and security. While one should not use a bank for a long-term investment plan, there are a variety of options for a shorter-term investment. The worst thing to do is to leave the money in a place where it earns nothing. Given current rates of inflation, cash will lose between 1 to 3 percent of its value every year. Therefore, if you keep money hidden in a mattress, you are actually losing as the value of money decreases!

Depending upon how soon the money is needed, banks offer a variety of options at a different interest rates. Here are some of the basic products offered by banks:

- **Checking Accounts**—These are convenient because one is allowed to draw checks on the balance at any time. Often, however, no interest is paid.
- **Checking Plus Accounts**—These are checking accounts with large minimum balances (usually over $1,000). They offer a small interest rate.
- **Savings Accounts**—This is the run of the mill bank account. Since the money is still very liquid, the interest rate offered is low.
- **Money Market Accounts**—These are accounts that usually require a large balance, but the interest rates are tied to other market rates. They are relatively liquid and sometimes may be withdrawn without penalty.
- **Time Deposits**—The most common form of this type of account is called a **CD** (or certificate of deposit). If you promise a bank that you will not withdraw the money before a set date, the bank will give you a higher interest rate . . . usually one to two percentage points higher. A minimum deposit is required, and CDs range from thirty-day to ten-year increments. When the **maturity date** comes (that is the day that you can cash in the CD without penalty), you get the amount that you invested, plus the accumulated interest. Beware that there are stiff penalties for the early withdrawal of principal from a CD, although interest can generally be withdrawn without penalty.

The Pressing Question

7. Draw a diagram that illustrates the relationship between the liquidity and yield of a short-term bank investment.

E. Long-term Savings

There are two main reasons to save money for the long term: to build a retirement fund and to afford your child's education. This section deals specifically with the first reason. With the current status of Social Security, the smart thing to do is to save for your own retirement. It may seem like overkill to begin saving right out of college, but even a modest savings plan can bring unbelievable returns by the time you hit your fifties. Even people who have modest incomes can retire with enormous wealth. The secret is discipline.

The other not-so-secret concept is **compounding** interest. This means that when you earn interest on an investment for one year, the borrower will pay you interest based upon the higher second-year amount. For instance, on a $10,000 account in the first year, at 10 percent interest, $1,000 is earned. In the second year, the borrower will pay the same interest rate on $11,000. Ten percent of $11,000 is $1,100. After two years, the investment has grown to $12,100. After five years, the original amount has increased to $16,105. In other words, the gross profit on the investment is $6,105. In the meantime, you did not do any work for the money (other than abstain from spending it). It was earned just the same.

Disciplined investors will continually put money into their **portfolio**—their collection of various investments. Over the span of thirty years, the goal is to keep putting in a small amount of money faithfully. Look to the chart below. Notice that at even at one hundred dollars per month, someone can save a great deal of money. No matter how much you are able to save, you should start as soon as you graduate from college. The earlier the start,

Year	Amount Invested	Account Value	Year	Amount Invested	Account Value
1	$1,200	$1,254	16	$19,200	45,083
2	2,400	2,634	17	20,400	50,845
3	3,600	4,151	18	21,600	57,184
4	4,800	5,820	19	22,800	64,156
5	6,000	7,656	20	24,000	71,826
6	7,200	9,676	21	25,200	80,263
7	8,400	11,897	22	26,400	89,543
8	9,600	14,341	23	27,600	99,751
9	10,800	17,029	24	28,800	110,980
10	12,000	19,986	25	30,000	123,332
11	13,200	23,239	26	31,200	136,920
12	14,400	26,817	27	32,400	151,866
13	15,600	30,753	28	33,600	168,306
14	16,800	35,082	29	34,800	186,391
15	18,000	39,844	30	36,000	228,167

Investing $100 per month is recommended by most financial advisors. As you get older, the amount should increase. This scenario represents a 10 percent yield.

the greater the returns. The money deposited in the first few years will be the hardest working money in the whole portfolio. Imagine the retirement you could have if you were to save $200 or even $300 per month.

How much will you need to retire? The answer to that question relies upon the lifestyle you wish to enjoy when you get older. Knowing what you know about budgets, could you live on $20,000 per year, or perhaps you need $50,000?

Basically, $100,000 will give you $7,000 to 10,000 per year when you retire. You'll need more than that.

Notice that different sums will earn greatly differing returns. If you choose to live a simple lifestyle, you will not need as much money. However, if you wish to live extravagantly, you should plan on saving aggressively. In the end, it is possible for someone to have a relatively modest income and still retire comfortably.

The Pressing Question

8. What are some of the possible opportunity costs involved in saving for a retirement? Give two specific examples.

F. Some Common Retirement Fund Options

While many people who are nearing retirement are finding out that they have not saved enough money for a comfortable retirement, younger people are noticing a disturbing trend. Demographically, the United States is getting older. Because a tremendous amount of babies were born between 1945 and 1960, there is a bulge in our population in the 40- to 55-year-old range. These **baby boomers** will begin to retire in the next ten years. When they do, they will place an unbelievable strain on our Social Security and Medicare programs. This trend has many younger adults, including Generation X, fearing the bankruptcy of these social programs. How people presently under the age of twenty will save remains to be seen.

Few people want to work their entire lives, so some safe and smart investing over the long haul will pay off.

Lifelong savings plans to which someone deposits money are sometimes called **annuities**. These plans invest their money in a variety of areas. Lately, many investors have been choosing the stock and bond markets. People pool their money together with an investment firm and have experts invest the entire fund; thus these are called **mutual funds.** Two of the more popular ways to save money are as follows:

- **Individual Retirement Accounts (IRAs)**—Not as popular as they used to be, IRAs offer a worker the opportunity to deduct money from his or her gross earnings. The money is then given to an investment firm. The appeal of a tax-free investment was lost in 1986 when Congress took the status away from most IRA accounts. However, Roth IRAs now allow citizens to invest money from their net income. When it is withdrawn at retirement age (59.5 years), any capital gain or interest income is tax exempt.
- **401(k)s**—These are the most popular retirement fund today. They allow one to take money out of one's gross income before the government taxes it.

The holder of a 401(k) is taxed on the money that is withdrawn at retirement. The beauty of these plans exists in the fact they may be **matching funds**. The corporation one works for will contribute what the employee contributes—sometimes more. For instance, if Jill decides to put $200 per month into her retirement fund, she is actually saving $400 per month because of the additional contribution of her company. Thus, 401(k)s are a win-win situation. They are cheaper than traditional pension plans for the company, and they accelerate the saving potential and profitability for the employee.

- **Pension Plans**—Pensions are usually a perk offered by companies. The organization involved will contribute money to a pension fund in the name of the employee. Upon retirement, the worker will receive a predetermined amount of money each month. Pension plans are not offered as much as they were twenty-five to thirty years ago. The real growth is in defined contribution plans and away from defined benefit plans. (Many of the former include 401(k) components.)

The Pressing Question

9. Which of the retirement options appears to be the most attractive to workers today? For what reasons do people prefer these plans?

G. Dealing with Insurance

Being a teenager, you probably have talked about car insurance with family or friends. If you know what your auto insurance costs every year, you understand how frustrating such an expense can be. Many times, when a young man or woman graduates from college, the monthly insurance premiums will often cost more than the car payment. While it seems unfair, there is good reason for the expense.

People buy insurance to reduce risk. In everything we do, there is considerable chance. In particular, businesses and individuals are responsible for their actions. They are **liable**. Every time you drive to school, each time you go out to dinner, and every time you buy something, bad things might happen. Insurance allows us the opportunity to control our chances. Companies that offer insurance operate on a basic formula:

FREQUENCY x SEVERITY = PREMIUM

Take, for example, the average teenage driver. He or she will get into more accidents than people of any other age group. And, when accidents occur, the accidents will be more costly. This explains why the insurance **premiums**, or the cost of buying a policy, is always most expensive for teenage drivers.

While your car policy premiums are exorbitant, your health insurance would be much more reasonable. Young people get sick far less often than people of other age groups. Better yet, when you do get sick, it is usually not serious, and therefore, it will cost less. So, while you are expensive to insure behind the wheel, your wellness is dependable enough to result in very affordable health insurance premiums.

Insurance is expensive, but it does offer peace of mind. Always make sure you know what you're paying for.

There are many options available in an insurance plan. When buying auto insurance, you may choose to pay for more coverage. Policies can range from a few thousand dollars of coverage to millions. Of course, if you choose the security of more coverage, you will have to pay higher premiums. Also, insurance companies can reduce the cost of insurance by giving the option of co-payments in the event of a claim. These payments are called **deductibles**. If you have a car accident that causes $3,000 dollars in damage to your car, and you have a deductible of $500, you will have to pay five-hundred dollars of the repair costs, while the insurance company will pay the remaining $2,500. However, because people who have one accident on record are a greater risk to get into another accident, your premiums may go up.

Insurance companies use two tools to calculate their figures. First, **demographics** study characteristics of human populations such as age, income, gender, distribution, and vital statistics. For instance, when you reach the age of twenty-five and/or get married, your car insurance costs will go down considerably. When you reach these milestones, you will enter a new demographic group. These groups statistically get into less accidents than the group you previously belonged to, so costs will go down. The only way to calculate statistics is to calculate massive amounts of data and numbers. With the help of an **actuary**, or a person who computes insurance premiums with collected data, companies try to estimate the chances that someone will make a claim and how much that claim would cost.

Insurance policies can be bought for just about anything. Businesses insure themselves against lawsuits and liability. You and I insure our cars, homes, boats, and yes, our lives. Life insurance guarantees a cash payment (of a predetermined amount) to the survivors of the holder of the policy. **Term life** policies expire after a set amount of years, usually ten to twenty. **Universal life** plans are usually a bit more expensive but accumulate in value like any other savings plan. They are valid as long as the **premiums** are being paid.

The Pressing Questions

10. Imagine that you own a small pizza shop. What different types of insurance would you need to buy?

11. How would an insurance company calculate the premium for such policies?

H. A Credit to Your Name

When it comes to borrowing money, the word **credit** describes the reputation one has built in his or her dependability in regard to paying back borrowed money. For instance, a fifty-year-old person who has bought several cars, two houses, and other items with millions of borrowed dollars never having missed a payment will have good credit. In other words, creditors, or people who lend money, would be more than willing to lend him money. On the other hand, someone who has a credit history of paying late or not paying at all will have difficulty borrowing money. Just think, to what sort of person would you be willing to lend money?

Banks and other creditors use the services of credit agencies to decide whether or not to lend someone money. These agencies keep track of people's tendency to pay back borrowed money. If people renege on a debt, the creditor will report them to credit agencies. When those people go to borrow again, they might be turned down. This **credit history** follows us for seven years. Look to the sample below.

When considering someone's credit health, financial institutions consider four aspects of an individual. These are known as the 4 Cs:

- **Credit History**—When money was borrowed in the past, how faithfully was it paid back?
- **Character**—Does the person have a criminal past?
- **Capacity to Pay**—What is the person's monthly income and can he or she handle a monthly payment schedule?
- **Capital**—How much money does the person have in the bank? Or does the person have capital resources that could be considered **collateral** (objects that can be handed over to the bank in the event that the person doesn't pay the loan)?

However, many people today borrow more money than they can afford to pay back. A major reason for this is the easy access people have to **credit cards**. These cards allow the holder to borrow money freely. Unfortunately, the money is lent at high interest rates—usually between fifteen to twenty percent. Credit cards are issued through and managed by banks. They work through massive computer systems operated by companies like MasterCard and Visa. While credit cards do afford holders a certain amount of financial freedom, they often get people into trouble.

When people are unable to pay a debt, it is called a **default**. Creditors then have the right to repossess the item that the lent money bought. If someone is unable to pay a **mortgage** (or a loan that bought land, buildings, or houses), a lender is then allowed to **foreclose**, or take back the property. Sometimes people will be unable to pay back any of the money they have borrowed. If this is the case, they are able to go to court and ask to have assets protected from their creditors. This legal declaration of one's inability to pay one's debt is known as **bankruptcy**. While most credit information follows us for seven years, a bankruptcy will be on our credit record for ten years.

COMMENT:

PUBLIC RECORD CERTIFICATION

THE REPORTING BUREAU CERTIFIES THAT: public records have been checked for judgements, foreclosures, garnishments, bankruptcies, tax liens, and other legal actions involving the subject(s) were obtained directly through the repositories used, or by direct searches, or a public records search firm other than the repository, or by all methods with the following results:

NONE

PUBLIC RECORDS LEARNED:

CREDIT HISTORY

CREDITOR							REMARKS						
ACCOUNT NUMBER	DATE VERIFIED	DATE OPENED	HIGH CREDIT	BALANCE OWING	AMOUNT PAST DUE	TERMS	ECOA	TYPE ACCOUNT MOP	HISTORICAL STATUS NO. OF MO's	30-59	60-89	90+	LAST PAST DUE
AMERICAN EXP													
00000000	01/97A	02/89	$0	$0	$0		I	OUR	48	0	0	0	
	03/96C												
COMMENT: CREDIT LINE CLOSED BY CONSUMER													
BNFICIL--BNCH													
00000000	04/93A	08/92	$455	$0	$0		I	I01	8	0	0	0	
	04/93C												
CENTURIONS&T													
0000	11/93A	03/89	$0	$0	$0		I	RUR	29	0	0	0	
	07/93C		$ 2K										
COMMENT: CREDIT LINE CLOSED BY CONSUMER													
CITIBK VISA													
000000000000	02/96A	11/89	$0	$0	$0		I	R01	48	0	0	0	
	10/95C		$ 4K										
COMMENT: CREDIT LINE CLOSED BY CONSUMER													
CITY LOAN													
000000000000	06/90A	06/89	$666	$0	$0	12M	I	I01	3	0	0	0	
	06/90P												

Keeping track of your credit is important. You may write or call one of the three major credit agencies in the country, such as Equifax, Trans Union, or Experian. Your record follows you for seven years. Businesses and creditors report any problems to the big agencies.

In bankruptcy court, there are three options to choose from. The judge will decide which is best depending upon the situation. They are as follows:

- **Chapter Seven**—The debtor is allowed to write off the outstanding debt. Taxes, alimony, and student loans must still be paid. Assets and personal holdings are sold to pay these off.
- **Chapter Eleven**—In these cases, an individual or business can delay payments to creditors while he or she undergoes a financial restructuring.
- **Chapter Thirteen**—Under these agreements, the debtor may keep all assets while paying back a percentage of each debt to various creditors. The plan is arranged by the court according to each situation.

While bankruptcies are a last resort for individuals or corporations, they can help the debtor survive financial difficulty. They are a very serious blow to a credit rating, and they can be overcome only with years of responsible spending.

The Pressing Question

12. How can a college student build a credit rating in order to finance a car after graduating?

If you can't pay your creditors, you must say so in court.

I. Buying Houses and Cars

Taxes are the second biggest expense paid by the American consumer. The first and third are houses and cars respectively. When people speak of the American Dream, it primarily means that someone will attain financial independence, a house, and a car or two. Because these are expensive items, most people have to borrow money in order to get them.

Getting both of these things will most likely involve borrowing money for you. The act of borrowing money over time and paying interest on it is known as **financing**. As you know, people who borrow money are very concerned with the annual percentage rate (**APR**) they will pay. Our national interest rates hinge upon the monetary policies of the Federal Reserve as well as the prevailing rate of inflation. Rates rise and fall according to this base rate. Among the interest rates that a smart consumer watches are

- **Discount Rate**—the rate charged by the Fed to its borrowers
- **Prime Rate**—the rate that banks charge large businesses and other banks for short term loans
- **Mortgage Rates**—These vary from bank to bank, but they tend to be the lowest offered to consumers. The duration of the loans range from five to thirty years.

- **Auto Loan Rates**—These are typically a bit higher than mortgage rates, and the length of the loan is typically three to five years.
- **Credit Card Rates**—usually the highest rates charged by banks (As discussed before, they are usually 15 to 20 percent per year.) These are unsecured loans.

As mentioned in Part 3, lending rates fluctuate according to the policies of the Fed. Currently, interest rates are very reasonable. Borrowing for a house will cost around 7–9 percent. Buying a car will cost around 10 percent.

What does a rate of 7.5 percent mean to a home buyer? To figure out a monthly payment, a creditor will **amortize** the loan amount. This is a loan in which each payment includes some amount for the interest (accrued the month before) and some amount for the principal (remaining balance). For instance, with a principal amount of $100,000 at an interest rate of 7.5 percent, the borrower must pay approximately $7,500 in interest in the first year of the loan. This breaks down to $625 per month in interest payments alone. The bank has specified how much of the payment is interest and how much is principal. As with most mortgages, the first several years are spent paying interest. In fact, this $100,000 loan could tally over $160,000 in interest payments by the end of a fifteen-year term.

Auto loans are also expensive when it comes to interest payments. A $20,000 car will cost nearly $24,000 with interest at prevailing rates in a sixty-month loan. It is advisable to negotiate the price when buying a car. Dealers will post a sticker price, but people rarely pay that price. They will gladly draw the price down several hundred dollars without much of an argument. It is smart to look in trade magazines, *Consumer Reports*, or buyer services for the real dealer invoice price. In fact, published invoice prices are often 3 percent higher than what manufacturers charge the dealer. This **holdback** is something most car sellers would rather you did not know about.

The last consideration in getting a car is the option to **lease** a car. In the past, leases were things reserved for businesses. However, with the rising price of cars, leases offer a nicer car for a lower monthly payment to individuals and/or families. The affordability comes from the fact that instead of financing the full price of a new car, a lease will finance the amount that the car will depreciate during the duration of the lease. For example, an $18,000 car will depreciate around 50 percent in three years. Therefore, $9,000 is financed over thirty-six months (around $300 per month). Buying the car would cost over $500 per month in the same time frame. On the other hand, at the end of the lease that had cost you almost $11,000, you have nothing for your money. In effect, a lease is a long term rental, so the value of the asset is zero at the end of the term.

The Pressing Questions

13. How much does the mortgage described on the left cost during one year?

14. If that person makes $56,000 per year, what percentage of his or her income is being occupied by housing payments?

J. Credit Cards

Most people who have to declare bankruptcy can pinpoint their downfall to a hefty credit card debt. As you get older, you will begin to experience the barrage of credit card offers. After finishing school, you may be offered thousands of dollars in credit and enticing introductory rates. As with any contract, make sure you read the fine print, especially in regard to interest rates, fees, and penalties.

The problem with credit cards is that they let the consumer get immediate gratification. Instead of having to save for that new stereo and TV, you can get it right away. Credit cards also operate on the concept of **revolving debt**. When a purchase is made on a credit card, the entire balance does not have to be paid off at the end of the month. In the meantime, the holder will be charged the high interest rates that go along with the credit card. This interest adds up very quickly.

Credit cards are convenient, but pose a danger to the unwary consumer who doesn't read the fine print in the agreement.

If you do not wish to carry large amounts of cash and still want the convenience that a credit card offers, there are two alternatives. A **charge card** like American Express will let you spend whatever you want interest free, but requests that the entire balance be paid at the end of the month. Another idea is to pay cash with an ATM or **debit card**. Many banks offer debit cards that are tied to your checking account and that feature a credit card logo on them. Using a debit card is the same as using cash, because the money comes directly from your checking account. Keep in mind not all checking accounts have this flexibility.

Here are some useful pieces of advice when it comes to credit cards:

1. Buy only what you can pay off at the end of the month.
2. Vigorously seek out new cards that offer low introductory rates and transfer outstanding balances.
3. Only buy goods that will last. Dinners and entertainment are fleeting. A TV, for example, can be enjoyed for years.
4. Be ashamed of yourself when you use them. A guilty conscience can keep you out of debt.
5. Get a card in college if one is offered. Buy a few small things for which you already have cash (like your schoolbooks). Pay off the balances right away. By doing this, you will establish a credit history of being a good risk. This will help once you graduate and go to make a major purchase.

Credit cards have become a major part of our financial culture. They offer freedom and convenience. Unfortunately, many people use them frivolously and get themselves into financial trouble.

The Pressing Question

15. What is the yearly and monthly interest charge to someone who has a $5,600 balance on a credit card that charges 17.5 percent APR?

K. Stock as an Investment

Recall Part 2's young entrepreneur Paul, who needed money to expand his lawn care business and tried to find investors. When he found a partner who was willing to use personal holdings to create something, the money that was offered can be considered a **real investment**. In other words, the money risked will help to create something new. Most investments made in America today are **financial**. Those are items that may earn money but create no new goods.

During the late 1990s, there was an enormous growth in the stock markets in the United States. More people felt comfortable putting their money in the market, and corporations have taken measures to become more profitable. Stock is an attractive investment because it offers the investor two different ways to make money. First of all, the stock may become more valuable and the holder can buy low and sell high. This is called a **capital appreciation**. Second, stock gives the holder a piece of ownership in the company. This means that the investor gets a share of the profits returned in cash in proportion to his or her ownership. This share of the profits is called a **dividend**.

Investors must decide on their financial goals when it comes to making a stock investment. There are many types of stock from which to choose. **Income stocks** are associated with profitable companies that offer steady dividends. People who buy **growth stock** plan to keep the stock for a long time and expect a large capital appreciation. Over the long term, their dividends may increase as well. Sometimes companies will offer an issue of **preferred stock**. This is stock that gives the investor a fixed share of the profits before common shares. These days, most stock transactions must be done through a brokerage house or Internet service.

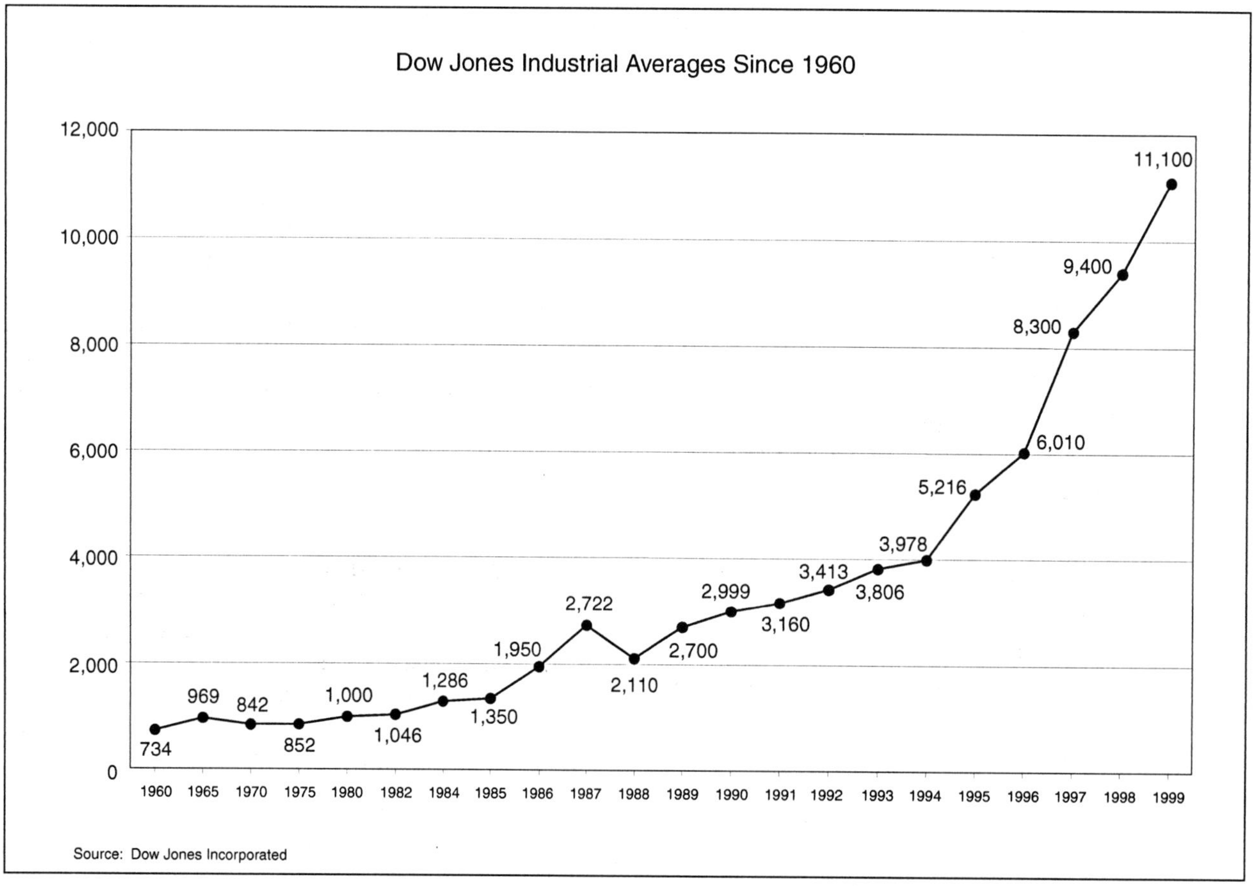

52-wk high	52-wk low	Stock	Div	Yield	PE Ratio	Vol	High	Low	Last	Change
79 ½	55 ½	Apcorp	2.46	4.5	8	1566780	55	53	55	+2 3/8
71 ¼	50 ¼	Citycom	3.60	5.1	9	34550	70	69	70	+1 ½
39 ¾	20 ½	Hesscom	0.13	.4	23	12400	31	30 ½	31	-½

Key

1 52 Week High—the highest price paid for the stock in the year
2 52 Week Low—the lowest price paid for the stock in the year
3 Stock—the company's name (sometimes the symbol)
4 Dividend—the annual return per year
5 Yield—the percentage return on the investment. It is dividing the annual dividend by the current price of the stock
6 Price-Earnings Ratio—the current stock price divided by the company's earnings per share. The lower the number, the better the value
7 Volume—the amount of shares that traded hands that day
8 High—the highest price gotten for the stock during the day
9 Low—the lowest price offered for the stock that day
10 Last—the last price offered per share that day
11 Change—the net change from the previous day's closing price

Stockbrokers buy and sell stock for a living. Usually, they work for a **brokerage house** that is a member of several stock exchanges. By having a **seat** on the exchange, the company is given the right to conduct transactions through that particular market. For every transaction made, the investor is charged a percentage (called a **commission**), anywhere from 1 to 5 percent, of each transaction or trade. With the onset of the internet, more people are using online services to trade stock. However, making money as a casual day trader is not that easy. Stock should be a long-term investment; day trading is much closer to gambling than it is to investing. Seeking the advice of a professional is best.

If you decide to buy one-thousand shares of IBM, you will need to conduct a transaction on the New York Stock Exchange (NYSE). You will be buying stock that has already been issued and held by several other investors. Because IBM is available to any investor, it is known as **common stock**. These types of transactions take place on a **secondary market**, because they have previously been issued.

Markets like the NYSE also provide a forum for companies to offer stock for the first time, also known as an **initial public offering**. Also working for brokerage houses are people called **investment bankers**. Their job is to decide how much a company's stock should sell for and how many shares should be offered. When initial offerings are made, the stock is usually sold to larger investment firms on a **primary market**.

Once you own a piece of a company, you will want to keep a close eye on how the company is doing. The company will contact you frequently to keep you up to date. They will send you a copy of their annual report. This will detail the profits, costs, debt, and future considerations of the company. Every day, investors watch their holdings closely in business sections of newspapers in the stock charts. Each category can tell a savvy investor something useful about the company's stock. (See sample above.) However, more information is needed than provided on this chart. Most investors do voluminous research before buying into a company.

As you look through a business section, you will notice that there are charts provided for thousands of companies on many different stock markets. In fact, each market dictates criteria that each company must possess before it can list itself on the exchange. Among the main national markets are

- **NYSE** (New York Stock Exchange)—This is most important market in the United

States. The biggest and oldest companies list their stock here. The trading takes place through the open outcry system and computers.

- **AMEX** (American Stock Exchange)—Also a large market, the AMEX caters to smaller industrial companies. It also uses the open outcry system. It should be mentioned that the AMEX and the NASDAQ merged as companies. However, they are still two separate markets.
- **NASDAQ** (National Association of Securities Dealers Automated Quotation System)—Smaller, unproven companies that want their stock offered nationally will go to this market. Also featured on this market are newer, high-tech firms like Intel and Microsoft. Investors still need to go through brokers, but there is no traditional trading floor.

Each of the markets has indicators which state how trading went that day. If you have ever watched the national news and noticed that they always quote how the stock markets did, you will notice that they usually just mention indexes. For the NYSE, the Dow Jones Industrial Average gauges the value of thirty companies and is the most widely quoted index in the country. The financial service company Standard & Poor compiles **S & P 500** by tracking the value of five hundred stocks instead of thirty. It contains NASDAQ stocks as well. It is approximately the fund largest capitalized companies (measured by their market value—total value of stock outstanding). The smaller markets also have indexes that are usually called **composites**.

In the past several years, the Dow has grown at a furious clip. People have rushed to the market to cash in on the hopes that their money will grow quickly. In 1991, the Dow hovered in the 2,000-point range. Remember that the Dow is merely an indicator of the market as a whole. However, stocks have skyrocketed in value lately. In January of 2000, the Dow reached new highs in the 11,400 point range. In the past, such **bull markets** (a period of increasing capital value) have always been followed by a **bear market** (a period of decreasing market value). The experts have been waiting for years for the markets to take a plunge. In fact, investors have endured large fluctuations in the past few years due to market volatility.

The Pressing Question

16. On the stock page shown, circle two companies that you recognize. For each company, detail how much the chart tells you about the state of the stock and activity of the stock.

The Dow Jones Industrial Average 30

1.	American Express	AXP
2.	Allied Signal	ALD
3.	Intel	INTC
4.	McDonalds	MCD
5.	Exxon	XON
6.	IBM	IBM
7.	The Home Depot	HD
8.	Hewlett Packard	HWP
9.	Citigroup	C
10.	General Motors	GM
11.	Wal-Mart	WMT
12.	Johnson & Johnson	JNJ
13.	Dupont	DD
14.	International Paper	IP
15.	Boeing	BA
16.	Merck	MRK
17.	United Technologies	UTX
18.	SBC Communications	SBC
19.	AT&T	T
20.	Coca-Cola	KO
21.	General Electric	GE
22.	Procter & Gamble	PG
23.	Phillip Morris	MO
24.	Disney	DIS
25.	3M	MMM
26.	J.P. Morgan	JPM
27.	Eastman Kodak	EK
28.	Caterpillar	CAT
29.	Alcoa	AA
30.	Microsoft	MSFT

L. The Bond Market

While stocks are popular investments, bonds are also very common. Unlike stocks, which offer ownership in a company, **bonds** are loans that investors make to governments and corporations. For instance, a bond issued by the Treasury Department is a loan to the U.S. Government which will promise to pay a certain interest rate over time. By going straight to the investor, the borrower gets a lower interest rate, and the lender gets a higher return. Bonds are the foundation of finance.

Bonds are not very easily understood. If you buy a $10,000 five-year bond at an interest rate of 10 percent, you will be paid $1000 for the first year of the agreement. For the following four years, an additional sum of one thousand is earned. The money will be paid by the borrower when the bond matures, or comes due. If the bond has a **maturity** of five years, the bond will be worth the original $10,000 at the maturity date plus the money earned.

Depending on the bond, the ways that you get your money can happen in a variety of ways. Sometimes you pay a fraction of the face value of a bond and the full amount is paid upon maturity. Sometimes you get an interest check in the mail once a month, quarterly, or annually. If you can think of an arrangement, it has most likely been done.

Common Bond Ratings

Investment Grade	Speculative Grade
AAA—Low Risk	BB
AA	B
A	CCC
BBB	CC—Very High Risk

There are several types of bonds available in the United States. A few of the more common are as follows:

- **Savings Bonds**—These can be bought for as little as $50. They have maturities of ten to thirty years. They are bought at a fraction of face value. They make great gifts.
- **Treasury Bonds**—The minimum investment is $1,000. The average investment duration varies.
- **Treasury Notes**—Maturity ranges from one to five years.
- **Treasury Bills**—These require a minimum investment of $10,000. They are held for a range of three to twelve months.
- **Corporate**—When a company needs to raise money, they may choose to sell stock, but more often they sell bonds. They operate in the same way as government bonds.
- **Municipal Bonds**—These are sometimes called "munies." They are simply bonds that are offered by local governments. They are especially enticing because they are exempt from Federal taxation.

Bonds offer businesses and governments an alternative to borrowing money from a bank. Instead, businesses and governments can go directly to investors.

When issued, bonds are given a credit rating just as an individual is rated when applying for a mortgage. Companies approach large agencies when they wish to issue bonds. The company is then assigned a rating according to its ability to pay back a loan. Large companies with large holdings of capital and high profits are a safer bet. Younger companies with no track record and bleak prospects may also issue bonds but will have to pay a higher interest rate. Bonds are rated by different companies. Moody's rates bonds from AAA to CC.

As you can see, bonds are lumped into two main categories. **Speculative grade** bonds tend to be risky, and investors may lose the money they loaned. **Investment grade** bonds are considered a much safer investment.

Because the United States has a two hundred-year-old spotless credit history, it has a rating of AAA, which means it has to pay less for the use of the money. Old solid companies may have ratings of A as do some dependable local governments. Companies on the brink of failure have a rating of C. If that company has some capital holdings, it can issue **mortgage bonds** which will give the investor the right to possess the company's land holdings, buildings, and, in some cases, equipment. If the risky company has no resources, it can issue **debentures,** which are bonds offered on nothing but the good name of the issuer.

Like stock, bonds can be traded on markets. When they are issued for the first time, bonds are sold on a **primary market**. However, someone who has held a bond for a certain length of time, may decide to sell it for a variety of reasons before it matures. If held to maturity, bonds offer a guaranteed return unless the issuer defaults. But, if a bond is taken to a secondary market to be sold to another investor, there is more risk involved. Look to the diagram that describes the situation.

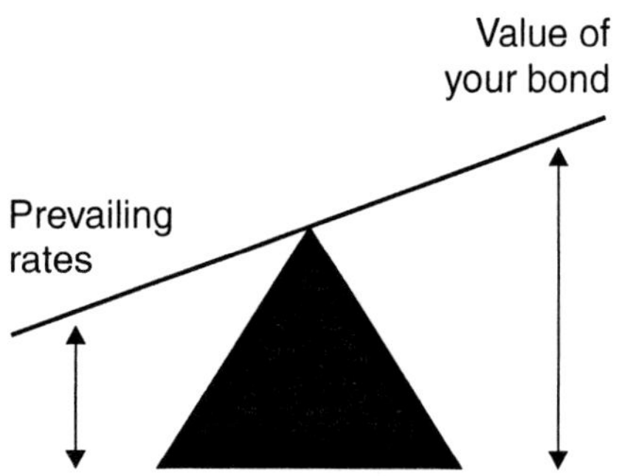

If you hold a 10 percent bond and want to sell it before maturity, the price you get will hinge upon prevailing interest rates. For instance, if people can buy 12 percent bonds when you hit the market, you will get far less than what you paid for the bond. On the other hand, if rates fall to 8 percent, you will get a premium for your bond. However, if you hold the bond to maturity, you will get the interest promised and your original investment back.

The Pressing Question

17. What types of bonds would you buy for

    a. a secure but quick investment?

    b. a high-rate of return?

    c. a savings plan for a newborn's college?

M. High-Risk Investments

Are you the gambling type? While some stocks and speculative grade bonds are considered risky, there are investments that can double in value in minutes. At the same time, they can become worthless just as quickly. Futures and options offer investors the right to buy and sell just about anything at a future date.

Commodities are articles of trade or commerce that can be transported, especially agricultural products. In the 1800s, farmers would experience wild fluctuations in price as harvest time came closer. All would rush to get their goods to market to garner the highest price. As time passed and more products arrived, prices would plummet.

To avoid this dilemma, farmers would sell their product to commodity traders months before harvest. The traders would then take the **"futures"** to a commodities exchange. Depending on the weather, world harvests, political conditions, and thousands of other factors, the unharvested product's price would fluctuate. This process continues on a grand scale in numerous places around the world. In the United States, the two largest markets are at the World Trade Center and the Chicago Board of Trade. On those frantic trading floors, the **hedgers** are people who hold options for several months and will eventually purchase the underlying commodity upon which the futures contract is based to secure a modest gain. On the other hand, **speculators** are buying and trading futures trying to make a quick buck either in the short or long term.

Stock options are contracts that convey to its holder the right, but not the obligation, to buy or sell shares of stock at a specific price on or before a given date. Options that give the holder the right to buy a stock are referred to as **calls**. If the value of the stock in question goes up, and you have the options at a low price, you can "call" your options in and get a discounted price. On the other hand, **puts** give the holder the right to make another party buy his or her holding. For instance, you hold some IBM stock which has climbed to $110 per share, and you wish to lock in your capital appreciation. When someone approaches you to sell you some puts, you agree. He sells you 1,000 puts of IBM at 110. For this, you pay him $2,000. This transaction benefits you, the holder, because you've guaranteed you can sell your shares for at least a predetermined price. The risk for the seller of the options is the chance that IBM falls in price and the holder of the options "exercises the option." This forces you to buy a stock at a higher-than-market price.

Many people you know have probably owned stock options at one time or another. They are not necessarily an investment of choice for the novice to the market. However, they can help those who own them.

If you own 1,000 shares of IBM that you bought at $100 per share, and the price has risen to $115, you may want to "lock in" your profits at the new price. In this case, you could sell options on your stock at the current price. If the price went down, the buyer would not want your stock. But, if the stock goes up, the buyer could take your stock at a discount price and you would lose the additional capital gain. It can all get quite confusing. Study your situation carefully before investing. When it comes to investing in futures and options, leave the job to the experts.

The Pressing Question

18. At what point in one's life is it safest to try a risky investment—closer to or further from retirement? Explain your logic.

The Purposes of Stock Options

	Call	Put
Definition	a contract in which a certain stock can be bought by the holder at a given price on a predetermined date	a contract in which a certain stock can be sold to a second party at a given price on a pre-determined date
Benefit to seller of contract	cash for each option	cash for each option
Benefit to holder	ability to buy a stock at a discounted price market price should rise	ability to sell stock at higher price if market price should fall

N. Rules of Thumb

There are two things worthy of note in personal finance. First, it does not take a genius to manage money and budget wisely. Second, few people in the United States actually do manage their money wisely. Here are some helpful tips for you:

1. Money is for saving, not for spending. Because of our consumer (TV-driven) society, most Americans spend money as soon as they have it and then borrow more to "keep up with the Joneses." Pay no mind to what others have. Living simply is the best and most financially sound way to go.
2. Always pay bills on time! Treat your credit with respect.
3. Always know where your money is. This sounds silly, but don't end up at the end of the month scratching your head and wondering where your money went.
4. Keep good records. Always save receipts and keep a file cabinet with important contracts, tax information, warranties, and other personal information.
5. Never have money sitting still. Money that earns no interest is actually losing value.
6. Always shop around. Get the best price on everything from mortgages, to cell phones, to home contractors. Get as many prices as possible and go with the best value.
7. Get good advice. Don't try to do this alone. Accountants, stockbrokers, and financial planners are expensive but often worth every penny due to the money they save you. Talk to your elders. Chances are they have experience from which you could benefit.
8. Buy smart, but buy quality. Don't waste your money on things that lose value like expensive cars and clothes. When you do buy, make sound choices on products that will last.
9. Deal with honest people. Always check references of the professionals in your life.

The Pressing Question

19. Why do so many Americans end up in financial trouble and eventually declaring bankruptcy?

Name____________________________

Date____________________________

The Language of Personal Finance

Directions: For each of the following sets of words, write a sentence that demonstrates an accurate understanding of the terms.

1. debit, bounced check, credit history

2. baby boomers, financial investment, mutual funds

3. interest, time deposits, liquidity

4. credit, bankruptcy, foreclosure

5 premiums, deductibles, demographics

6. prime rate, revolving debt, credit rating

7. real investment, dividend, capital appreciation

8. common stock, preferred stock, growth stock

9. bonds, primary market, maturity

Name________________________

Date________________________

10. investment bankers, debentures, secondary market

11. futures, speculators, hedgers

12. stock options, 401(k), income stock

13. default, credit rating, retirement

14. Dow, munies, IRAs

15. checking account, balance, credit

Name____________________________

Date____________________________

My Checkbook

Directions: Fill out the check register below with the information provided. The dates are not in order, so you must rearrange them and place them accordingly.

April 20	check 579 for car insurance $356.77
April 19	withdraw $60
April 19	ATM fee of $1.50
April 16	automatic deposit for $707.32
April 22	check 580 for gas bill $44.67
April 12	ATM fee of $1.00
April 13	check 578 for electric bill $56.98
April 19	auto debit for $28.66
April 18	service fee of $7.50
April 15	check 577 for car payment $184.79

Since this statement, you have done the following things:

withdrawn $50

written check 581 to the BMV for $55

written check 582 to your mom for $75

spent $47.78 at Franklin Music Store with debit card

The initial balance is $312.11. What is the ending balance?

Number	Date	Description	Debit	✓	Fee	Credit	Balance

Name__________________________

Date___________________________

My Budget

Directions: Fill in the first column of the following chart with figures that you think you will pay per month when you first enter the "real world." Then go home and inquire as to how much your parents or guardians pay for these things. In class, we will fill in the last column on the second day of the lesson.

Note to parent or guardian: Please feel free to be vague or withhold information from your child. An estimate is sufficient, of course.

Yes, my child did converse with me. Signature ______________________________________

Monthly Expenses	Your Estimate	Your Folks	Your Upcoming Reality
Housing			
Electric bill			
Gas bill			
Water			
Cable			
Phone			
Car			
Car insurance			
Groceries			
Gas for car			
Health/Hygiene			
Savings			
Clothes			
New stuff			
Student loans			
Entertainment			
Totals			

________________ 1. Add up the third column.

________________ 2. Multiply that number by 12.

________________ 3. Multiply line two by 1.30.

________________ 4. That is what you need to make every year.

Name____________________________

Date____________________________

You and Your Loans

Part A.

Directions: Follow the steps in both sections to estimate a payment.

Mortgage Payments

__________ 1. Estimate value of house to nearest $10,000 increment.

__________ 2. Divide that number by 10,000.

__________ 3. Multiply the answer to number 2 by $100.

__________ 4. The answer gives you an approximate house payment at an 8 percent, thirty-year mortgage.

Car Payments

__________ 1. Estimate the value of the car to the nearest $5,000 increment.

__________ 2. Divide that number by 5,000.

__________ 3. Multiply the answer to number 2 by $100.

__________ 4. That is the estimated car payment at 10 percent for five years.

Part B.

Directions: Answer the following questions.

1. What does it mean when a commercial talks about "5.9 percent financing?"

2. How long is the typical car loan?

3. How long is the typical home mortgage?

4. Why are interest rates higher for car loans?

Name______________________

Date______________________

5. What is the current average rate for a home mortgage, auto loan, credit card?

6. Realtors speak of "PITI" as the principal + interest + taxes + insurance one pays monthly to the holder of a mortgage. Define the components of "PITI."

   Why do holders of mortgages make their customers pay them the tax and insurance?

7. If you have a payment due on the first with a two-week grace period, why should you wait until the fifth or sixth of the month to mail your payment?

8. Equity is the amount of money you've paid on your house. What is the equity if you've paid half of the principle on a $150,000 mortgage and the house is currently worth $220,000?

   What is a home equity loan?

9. How much do mortgage lenders expect you to have as a down payment?

Name________________________

Date________________________

What could you give a bank in exchange for a lower interest rate?

10. Escrow is the amount you have to pay for taxes and insurance. Which is usually more expensive?

11. Using the formulas from the top of the page, what would the approximate payment be on a house costing $250,000? $80,000? $135,000?

What would the approximate payment be on a car costing $40,000? $15,000? $25,000?

12. What is the interest for the first year on a $100,000 mortgage at 8.25 percent? What is that monthly?

Name______________________

Date______________________

The Language of Wall Street

Directions: Translate the following phrases into language anyone could understand.

1. "The Dow closed down three points in heavy trading today."

2. "The market liked what was going on in Washington."

3. "Prices plummeted as nervous investors took part in a sell-off."

4. "The bond market responded positively to the news from the Fed."

5. "The Dow dipped drastically on bad news from the government on inflation figures."

6. "IBM finished up three points due to good news about third-quarter profits."

7. "The latest inflation and unemployment reports were well reflected on Wall Street."

8. "The Dow reached an all-time high, while the smaller markets registered only moderate gains."

9. "Apple finished up seven points amid rumors of higher dividends."

10. "Investors frenzied in a pre-holiday buy-up, reacting to good news from London and Tokyo."

11. "Gainers led losers today three to one."

12. "Large-cap stocks led today's rally as the blue chips soared."

13. "The market went in the tank today in a burst of profit-taking by investors."

14. "Analysts warned of rough times as IBM showed poor earnings in their latest quarterlies."

15. "The bears are predicting a correction in the market as big board trading slumped."

16. "Cyclical stocks got hit hard after some harsh words by the Fed Chairman."

17. "The bulls were running today on Wall Street after good news from the labor department."

Name________________________

Date________________________

Investing

Directions: Place the investments in the appropriate spot on the risk pyramid. Then answer the questions that follow.

savings accounts
junk bonds
mutual funds
blue chip stock
money market funds
futures
treasury bonds
options
growth stocks
corporate bonds
high-rated munies
CDs
rental real estate
speculative stocks
savings bonds

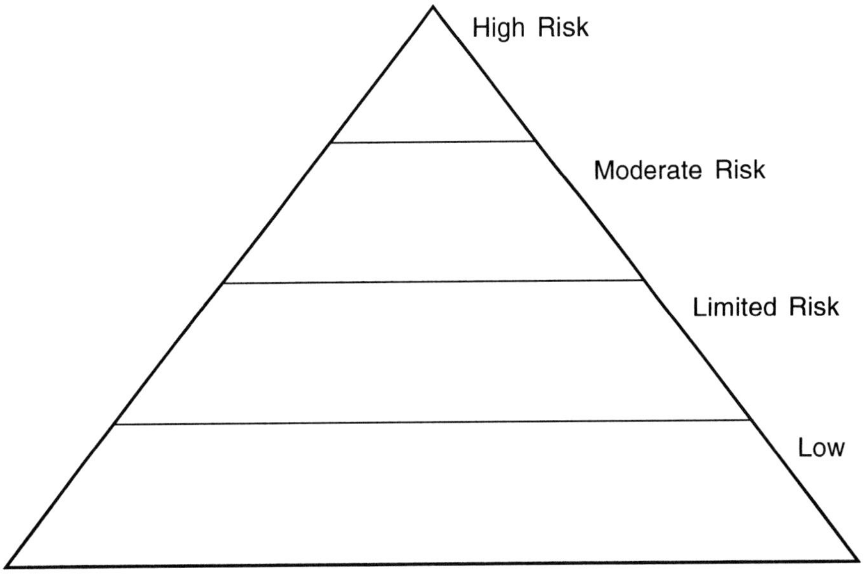

1. a. What would you invest if you had an aggressive investment strategy?

   b. What would you invest if you had a conservative investment strategy?

2. Use the two circles below to create pie charts for the same investor at two different times in his or her life. What should he or she be investing in?

Age 25 Age 65

3. Are futures a good way to save for a retirement?

4. Why should people take advantage of their 401(k) programs?

5. What does it mean to have money in a tax-deferred annuity?

6. What do economists mean when they use the terms *short-term* versus *long-term*?

Name________________________

Date________________________

Reading a Business Page

Directions: Using the business page that you brought to class, fill in all of the following information.

1. Write the date of your paper.

2. List the main sections of your business page.

3. List the five biggest stories of the day.

4. What sorts of ads do you see in the paper?

5. Name one article that has to do with
   a. scarcity
   b. government
   c. labor
   d. investors
   e. consumers
   f. important statistics

6. Find the price of
   a. two types of bonds
   b. two futures
   c. gold
   d. five company stocks
   e. prime rate
   f. discount rate
   g. five mutual funds
   h. five foreign exchange rates

Name________________________

Date________________________

The Challenge

Directions: For the next several weeks, you are being given an imaginary nest egg of $100,000. The object is to invest in three companies that you pick from the NYSE, AMEX, or NASDAQ markets. Over the duration of the assignment, you are to catalogue its price on sixteen days including the first and last day of the competition. They do not need to be consecutive days, just as long as you keep an eye on the situation.

	Date	Stock 1	Stock 2	Stock 3
Number of shares bought				
Original price				
Initial investment				
Day 2				
Day 3				
Day 4				
Day 5				
Day 6				
Day 7				
Day 8				
Day 9				
Day 10				
Day 11				
Day 12				
Day 13				
Day 14				
Day 15				
Price on last day (Day 16)				
Last price x shares bought				
Profit or loss				

Part 6
Global and Ethical Perspectives

Questions to Consider

1. How do honest people make it in the world of business?
2. Why is there poverty?
3. Why are other countries poor and the United States so rich?
4. Is free trade a good thing for the global economy?
5. How will the United States do economically in the next one hundred years?
6. Why did communism fail in Russia?
7. Is our economic system fair?
8. Is socialism a more humane form of economy?

Terms You Need in Order to Read

Ethics
Morality
Poverty
Free trade
Productivity
Socialism
Capitalism
Economy

Name________________________

Date________________________

Global and Ethical Perspectives

Directions: Read the selection, and answer the Pressing Questions as you read. Be prepared for class discussion.

A. Economic Power of the United States Today

Consider for a moment the place that the United States has in the world. Some people might call us the most powerful nation on the planet. We are often called the "leaders of the free world." Our nation's influence has developed over the past two centuries. Our power does not come from the fact that we have guns and bombs; it comes from our strong economy.

The average person living in the United States will produce over $30,000 per year. This high **per capita gross domestic product** means that we produce a massive amount of goods and services every year. When there is more produced and not consumed, more wealth is created. This will dictate a higher **standard of living,** or economic well-being for our citizens. Because there is more produced, there is more to be divided among the populace. If we did not produce as much, there would be less for us to have, and our standard of living would diminish.

Think about American teenagers for a moment. Many are currently considering going to colleges that cost more money per year than some people in the world will see in a lifetime. Many wake every day in a dwelling that is climate controlled, relatively safe from crime, and furnished with an assortment of electronic conveniences. In the morning, there is food in the refrigerator and clothes in the closet to choose from. In some cases, there is a car to drive to school. American teenagers' weekends are filled with movies, games, and the company of friends. Best of all, they are given the choice of determining their futures. Life in America is extremely pleasant by the standards of our world. How close do you come to the scenario above? Remember that most people in the world do not have adequate housing, plumbing, or even electricity.

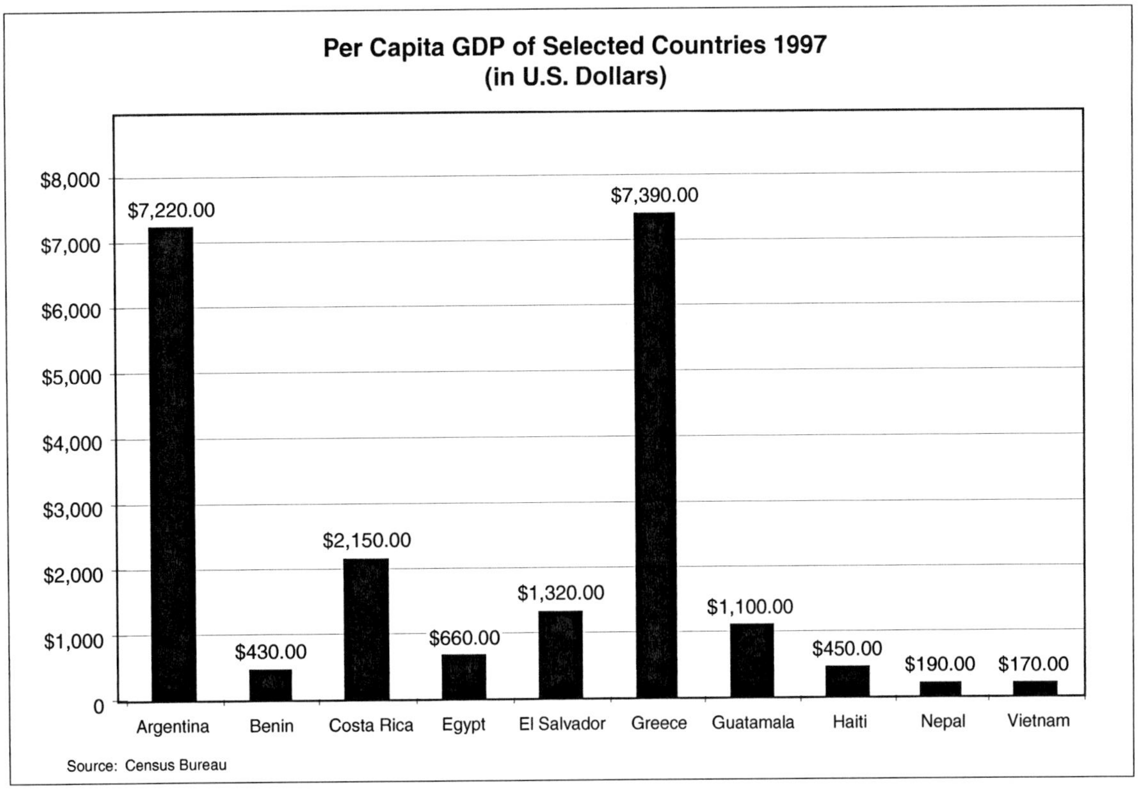

Look to the chart on the previous page that lists the per capita GDP of selected nations. Notice that the United States is far more productive than many others. Imagine for a second what life must be like for a citizen of a country that has a per capita GDP of a few hundred dollars per year. Are children in these countries told that they can grow up to be the leader of their country someday? Do they even go to school? Do they have electricity at all? Do they have enough food?

The Pressing Question

1. List five items that you would not have if they were not provided for you by someone else.

B. Problems in Less Developed Countries

The term **less developed countries** refers to nations that are severely underdeveloped, have low productivity, and whose population is impoverished. These countries can be found in Latin America, Africa, Eastern Europe, and Asia. By describing a country as **underdeveloped**, it means that it lacks industry, infrastructure, and economic resources. These countries also contain over 75 percent of the world's population.

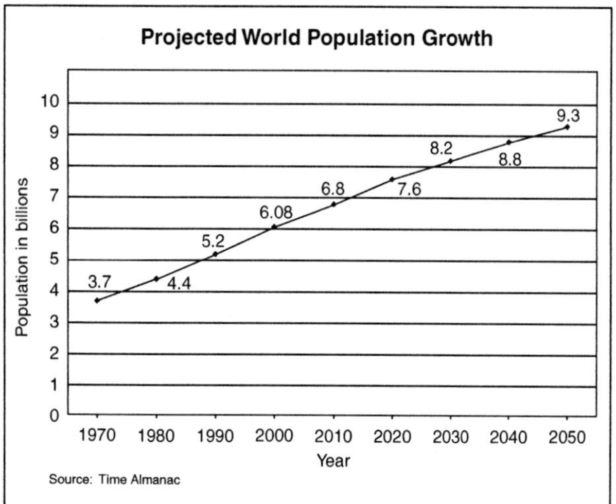

Why can't they develop? Why don't they get their acts together and begin to prosper? Actually, there are several reasons that keep less developed countries in the state they are in:

- **Lack of Capital**—Poor countries do not have much human-produced wealth—capital goods. Without capital, the country cannot build new factories or businesses. Their governments lack the money to build the necessary roads, power plants, water systems, and airports necessary to allow the economy to grow. This lack of infrastructure will not allow businesses to start or expand. People do not save money or invest it, because they need it to live. Furthermore, foreign investors shy away from many less developed countries, because they fear political instability or the lack of infrastructure needed to conduct business.

  The biggest issue is often political corruption—politicians getting rich at the expense of the common person. That leads to an apparent "lack of capital." Also, often the controlling political party does not want to educate the masses—and education is a primary driver of economic growth. No education equates to no growth.

Top Per Capita GDP by Nation

Country	Per Capita GDP 1997
Switzerland	$43,479.93
Japan	$42,736.09
Denmark	$36,656.21
Norway	$36,206.64
Singapore	$31,600.89
Germany	$30,493.78
Austria	$29,485.56
United States	$29,142.63
Belgium	$28,002.34
France	$27,228.94
Netherlands	$27,179.38
Sweden	$26,941.52

Source: Census Bureau

Some countries are better at making high-tech products and manufactured goods. Other less developed countries should stick to agricultural goods. They have an advantage there.

- **Lack of Natural Resources**—Many countries simply do not have the natural resources to develop. A country like Mali or Oman suffers from a desert climate that inhibits adequate agriculture. Furthermore, they both lack sufficient mineral resources to produce new goods. While a country like Japan has few natural resources, it has the manufacturing base that processes foreign raw materials into saleable goods.
- **Overpopulation**—In many countries, children insure that the parents will have extra labor or income when they begin to work. Often, the family relies on **subsistence agriculture**. This means that they must grow the food that they eat. They spend most of their time tending to a farm. Children can be a great help, but unfortunately, food is sometimes scarce. Even worse, there is little time to produce other goods, which leaves the family with no hope for economic improvement. The highest population growth rates are in less developed countries.
- **Lack of Skilled Workers**—The education systems of many countries cater to too few of the population. Also, a "brain drain" of highly educated people to developed countries takes place. Because of this, the country will lack the skilled workers needed to produce goods that can be sold to other countries.
- **Historical Reasons**—Many less developed countries were at one time colonies of a Western power. India, for instance, spent hundreds of years under British rule. Any economic development that happened benefited England. (There were *some* benefits to India, but distribution was surely inequitable.) Most capital did not stay in India to help it grow. Because of this trend, numerous less developed countries have languished with terrible economies as the European governments left.
- **Political Instability**—In one country in Africa, the Democratic Republic of the Congo (formerly Zaire), Dictator Mobutu Sese Seko made deals for decades with foreign companies that used Zaire's limited resources to benefit the foreigners. In turn, Mobutu's bank accounts were stocked with huge amounts of cash that helped him maintain a fearsome military. In many other countries, the threat of revolution scares away foreign investors.
- **Social Obstacles**—In some countries, society is structured according to strict social or class divisions. In Iran, the theocratic government restricts rapid economic growth. The politicians protect themselves from consumerism for fear of losing religious purity.

The United States hopes underdeveloped countries will grow economically. While the factors listed above are difficult to overcome, even small countries can become valuable trading partners. We hope someday that a country will develop to the point where its citizens will have the resources to buy our products. In that case, we both benefit.

To help countries in development, the United States spends billions of dollars in foreign aid. This spending has come under attack in recent years. Some people feel that it is wrong to send money to other countries when it can be spent on United States citizens.

The Pressing Question

2. If you were in charge of helping a less developed country develop, what are three pieces of advice you would give?

Trade with foreign countries impacts every part of the United States. We will continue to become more dependent on trade with other countries in the future.

C. Free Trade or Not Free Trade

In the 1992 presidential election, there was a hot debate about **NAFTA** (North American Free Trade Agreement). In this treaty, Canada, Mexico, and the United States agreed to do away with economic barriers between them. Chiefly, this meant the reduction of **tariffs**, or the taxes countries place on imports. Candidate Ross Perot feared that American companies would quickly move plants down to Mexico in the search of cheap labor. He warned that we all would hear "a giant sucking sound" of jobs leaving for Mexico. However, since its inception, NAFTA has had mixed results for the United States. Some jobs have left, but the lower prices our products have in Mexico have created higher sales and increased profits for some domestic industries. Free trade grew more popular as the twentieth century came to a close. Is it a good idea? You must decide for yourself.

To get a better understanding of how nations interact economically, it is important to note that certain countries specialize in the production of certain products. For instance, Brazil can produce coffee more cheaply and efficiently than the United States. It is said that Brazil has the **absolute advantage** in this area. It is better for Brazil to make coffee than computers. It is better for the United States to devote its resources to the production goods other than coffee.

A nation must also consider the **comparative advantage** to producing a specific product. This refers to the ability of one nation to produce a good at lower opportunity costs relative to the same products in another country. For instance, both country X and country Y have the ability to produce both shoes and stereos. If they devote all their resources to stereo production, X can make 1,000,000 and Y can make 100,000. When it comes to shoes, X can produce 200,000 and Y can produce 100,000. When comparing the output in ratios, stereos are made at 10 to 1 between X and Y, and shoes are made at a ratio of 2 to 1. Clearly, X is the bigger economic force. However, when comparing the two countries together, it is advisable for country Y to compete in the shoe market. When the two products are put side by side, they are more likely to succeed in the shoe market. By specializing in the product they can produce more efficiently, both country X and country Y can make the best use of its available resources.

It is in the best interest of a country to export its products to other nations. The population of the United States can buy only so many cars, but by opening new markets, our auto industry can prosper and hire more people. Our government realizes this and can use many devices to control the flow of products across our borders. Ideally, it is better for a country to **export** more goods than it **imports**. This is a situation called a **trade surplus**. Unfortunately, the United States currently imports a great deal more than we export—**a trade deficit**. This is measured in dollars, and in recent years, it usually ranges in the tens of billions. If others are willing to hold our debt—both public and private—then as a

Trade Affiliation	Explanation
European Union	An agreement among several European countries to eliminate border tariffs and duties and eventually have one currency.
North American Free Trade Agreement	The 1993 treaty that created a unified market connecting the U.S., Mexico, and Canada.
Latin American Free Trade Agreement	A trade agreement meant to alleviate trade restrictions between South and Central American countries.
General Agreement on Tariffs and Trade	An international organization that creates a forum for negotiating tariffs.
G-8	The eight biggest economic nations that periodically get together to discuss trade and economic issues.

country we will run a long-run deficit, since we purchase other countries' goods and services with our debt—including our currency. The $100 bill is the most popular form of savings in many countries. Why? Because it is better to create goods and sell them than to rely on someone else to produce them, our government may place tariffs on imports. While this could be a good source of revenue for the government and will help to protect industries on which competitive imported products have tariffs placed, other countries may do the same to our products. This could result in a trade war where nations escalate their tariffs as to restrict any trade between countries. Worst of all, an **embargo** may be used to cut off trade altogether.

The threat of trade wars and economic disputes have prompted many countries to turn to free trade agreements. With lower tariffs between two countries, they hope that products will become more affordable and sales will increase. The chart above shows some of the more prominent free trade agreements in the world today.

With the growth of the Internet and the wide availability of telecommunication, more foreign companies are doing business and opening factories in countries other than their own. These multinational corporations (MNCs) will continue to be a growing force and influence in the world. This is sure to keep the debate about free trade alive and well.

The Pressing Question

3. How might a large trade deficit be bad?

D. Socialism in the World Today

When Mikhail Gorbachev dissolved the communist party in 1990, the Soviet Union ceased to exist and Russia as a single nation emerged. This ended fifty years of limited diplomacy and military threats between the United States and Union of Soviet Socialist Republics. This cold war not only had a constant threat of nuclear conflict but also pitted the economic theories of communism against capitalism.

While private interests own the factors of production in a **capitalist** economy, **socialism** describes a wide range of economies where the government owns some of or all of the means of production. Socialism was the brainchild of two men, Friedrich Engels and Karl Marx. In the mid-1800s, when the industrial revolution was taking hold in Europe, Marx and Engels were dismayed at the widening gap between the rich and the poor. They believed that history was a story of the struggle between those who own the factors of production and those who do not. They wished to see a society where everyone had approximately the same amount of goods, where there was an absence of class differentiation, and where the government worked to create an equitable economy. To bring about this new society, the Communist Manifesto called for "workingmen of the world" to unite in a revolution.

While Marx never envisioned that his ideas would grow into a nation like the former Soviet Union, he did believe that after the revolution, there would be a need for somebody to guide the country into its utopian future. Immediately following the revolution, he called for a dictatorship of the **proletariat,** or the working class. These worker/leaders would step down eventually. But, as human nature would dictate, those leaders the Communist Party—decided not to forfeit their powers and a more traditional dictatorship developed. Vladimir Lenin called the society he helped to create "communism" because the controllers of the economy were all members of the Communist Party. The economic system of the old Soviet Union differed greatly from the ideas of Karl Marx just as the modern capitalist United States differs from that envisioned by Adam Smith.

However, a key to any Marxist society is the concept of **central planning**. This means the government decides how much of each product should be produced, how resources are used, and how citizens should work and live. Look to the supply and demand graph for toasters. Do you notice anything peculiar about the market for toasters in a communist country? How likely is it that central planners will be able to forecast accurately the price and quantities at which the market will clear?

In turn-of-the-century Russia, there was a class of nobles who owned much of the wealth and a class of peasants that lived in dire poverty. **Vladimir Lenin**, a leader of a socialist club called a Soviet, led a revolution to overthrow the czar (king). of Russia. In 1917, the revolution succeeded in dethroning the czar. Lenin and his leaders began to create what they hoped would be a perfect socialist state. Unfortunately, when Lenin died, his successor was a paranoid tyrant named **Josef Stalin**. For almost thirty years, Stalin dictated the direction of every aspect of Soviet society. A socialist state that is controlled by one person is called **authoritarian socialist**.

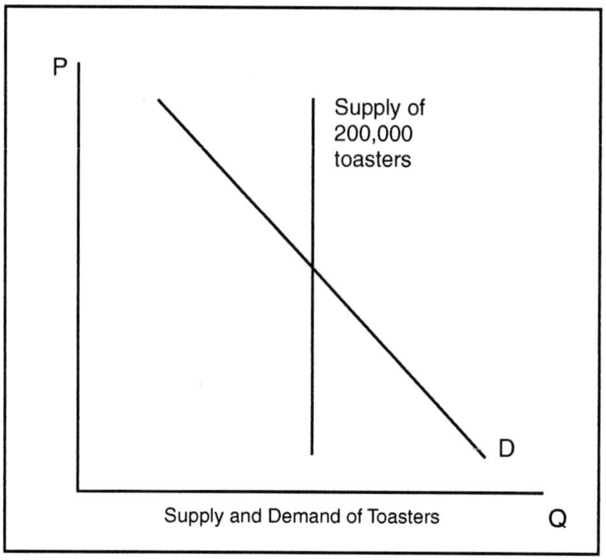

Socialism does exist in other forms around the world. In Sweden, for instance, people retain the basic democratic rights like free speech and public elections while the government plays a key role in the planning of the economy. This is called **democratic socialism**. The Swedish government controls about 10 percent of the country's industry while the rest is owned by private interests. Most notable in a democratic socialist state is the level of taxation. Over one-half of the country's income is handed over to the government. With this money, the public benefits from a vast network of social programs like health insurance, free education, subsidized housing, and retirement benefits. Because of this, Swedes enjoy one of the highest standards of

Communist Revolutions of the Twentieth Century

Country	Year(s)
USSR	1917
North Korea	1947
China	1949
Vietnam	1950s–1975
Cuba	1959
Cambodia	1975

living in the world. On the other hand, tax revenue cannot keep up with the rising cost of the social programs, and the demand for higher wages is a constant cause of worry.

While the Soviet Union has disbanded, authoritarian socialism still exists in countries like North Korea, China, and Cuba. Democratic socialism exists in some form in France, Great Britain, Germany, and Spain. It also exists in many less developed countries like Mozambique, Algeria, and Tanzania. There is much talk in European countries like France that socialism is stifling economic growth. There is also considerable worry that the former Soviet-bloc countries will revert back to the hard-line communism that they depended on in the past. There are efforts by the United States to help these emerging markets like Russia, Romania, and Bulgaria to adjust to life under capitalism.

Karl Marx believed that socialism was a way to stop the cold nature of economics. In other words, he truly believed that it was unfair that some people should live in riches and luxury while others lived in squalor. Many Americans believe that socialism is inherently flawed as an economic system and that is the reason the Union of Soviet Socialist Republics ceased to exist. Despite this, socialism still exists and is a force to be dealt with and understood.

The Pressing Question

4. Name three ways in which the United States is not a pure capitalist country.

5. Recall the definition for capitalism. Name three ways the United States is capitalist.

E. Being Good and Honest Out There

In recent years, there have been some disturbing trends in the United States. Companies have engaged in massive lay-offs of their workers to save money and to increase the value of their stock. While they have used words like "downsizing, streamlining, cutbacks, paring-down, and cutting-the-fat" to describe their activity, it all amounts to nothing more than firing people. It begs the question: Is there any moral commitment between employee and employer?

Most of the large corporations in the United States today are publicly owned. Stockholders apply pressure to the men and women (officers) to increase the profits of the company. In the end, labor is often the greatest expense of a company. Workers are turned loose as many factories are closed and production is moved to other regions or countries where labor is much cheaper. This is a dilemma for many people running large companies. Investors put hard-earned money into companies in the hopes of financial gain, but what becomes of these workers who lose their jobs?

Throughout your life, you have heard cliches like "it's a jungle out there," "kill or be killed," and "survival of the fittest." Some believe that to succeed in business and in many other professions, they may treat people in any way they see fit as long as it gets them advancement and/or profit. Companies purposely pollute the environment because it would mean higher profits. In the past, some businesses fired employees after years of service only a few months before their retirement to avoid paying the full retirement benefits. Unfortunately, these types of stories are commonplace.

For the past few years, many business schools have added a required course on ethics for their students. The fact of the matter is that when people lie and cheat, there are going to be victims. While the profit motive and greed can create new business growth, they can lead people to do dishonest things. Money cannot be the answer to your happiness. It may solve problems temporarily, but if you are unhappy with who you are, money will not change that. Treating people badly is unethical and it is bad business.

Ethics are the rules and standards that govern our conduct. Each profession has a specific set of rules that must be followed. For instance, psychiatrists are never allowed to divulge a patient's thoughts with other people. Defense attorneys must always give a defendant the best defense possible. Doctors take an oath to the effect that they will treat all people and never do harm to human beings. Many times, occupations require the employee to take an oath of conduct or sign a contract that dictates certain behavior. Ethics are not cut in stone. There are no easy answers, and the rules people agree to sometimes make work difficult. You must decide for yourself what is honest and what is not. You must stand for something in your life.

It can be argued that a person is most defined by the nature of his or her relations to other people. For instance, a doctor is one who heals. A parent is one who nurtures another human being to adulthood. A teacher is one who imparts knowledge. A stockbroker is one who assists people in various financial transactions. Each of these positions can be noble, ordinary, or harmful. Whenever selfishness or dishonesty creep into any of our life choices and roles, it will be at the expense of another human being.

The Pressing Question

6. What types of things could a business do to improve society?

F. Poverty in the United States

The United States is the most affluent country in the world. Why are there still people in the United States who live in poverty? With so much being produced and so much being consumed, one would think that there would be enough prosperity for everyone. As things stand now, 13 percent of the people of the United States live under the poverty line. The government considers that a family of four that makes less than $16,600 per year is living in poverty.

Contrary to an old saying, money is not the root of all evil. It depends on what you do with it. If something is wrong, it is wrong and someone should not profit from it. It is possible to treat people well, conduct yourself with dignity, and be an honest person while living a comfortable lifestyle.

In our society, the wealth created by our industrial growth in the twentieth century has brought about a voracious appetite in Americans for consumer goods. This constant accumulation of goods with the belief that they will bring happiness or benefit is called consumerism. People accumulate material wealth around them because they believe they need it, or they believe it will make them happy. Companies skillfully advertise and market their products to us. Secondly, material goods do make us happy in the short-run, but ask yourself, "Do I really need all this stuff?" Then ask, "If I buy something more sensible, what could be done with the remaining money?"

People have the right to spend their money the way they wish. However, it is never a good idea to squander money. If a person drives a $60,000 car, could they have gotten by with one that costs a third of that? What could they have done with the $40,000 they saved? It could have been given to a charity, invested in a bond or stock, or used to help a family member. People waste their money because they buy status symbols. They are forms of what some people consider to be **conspicuous consumption.** At the turn of the nineteenth century, sociologist Thorstein Veblen coined this phrase to describe overt displays of wealth.

While some have so much, others in the United States have far less. Psychologically, poverty in our country is far worse than in other countries. **Relative poverty** is the condition that people feel when comparing their lives with others in their society. Because of our mass media, people are constantly exposed images of what money can buy and how other people live. This situation makes the emotional impact of poverty that much worse. Seeing others live in comfort and luxury as you are in a dire situation will breed feelings of inadequacy, discontent, and resentment. On the other hand, sometimes when comparing impoverished Americans to other poor people around the world, the **absolute poverty**, or direct comparison between them, is less severe. In any case, wherever people live in poverty, crime rates and child abuse are more likely to be higher. This makes life even more difficult.

In the last twenty years, about 13 percent of the U.S. population has continued to live in poverty. While many people have attained some social mobility, it is difficult to rise because people who live in poverty begin to develop a **culture of poverty**. This culture is highlighted by apathy and hopelessness. People who are raised in this environment feel as though there is no point to trying to better themselves. Many times their lives have been touched by violence, crime, abuse, and degradation. While many people in America experience temporary bouts with poverty, there are generations of our citizens who live with it constantly.

When looked at from the outside, attitudes of apathy are hard to understand, especially if one has had privilege and opportunity. But imagine that instead of growing up in a home where people told you how wonderful you were, you grew up where people treated you terribly. Your schools and neighborhood did not manage to grant you any hope either. While these situations are not excuses, they make accomplishment in the face of poverty that much more significant.

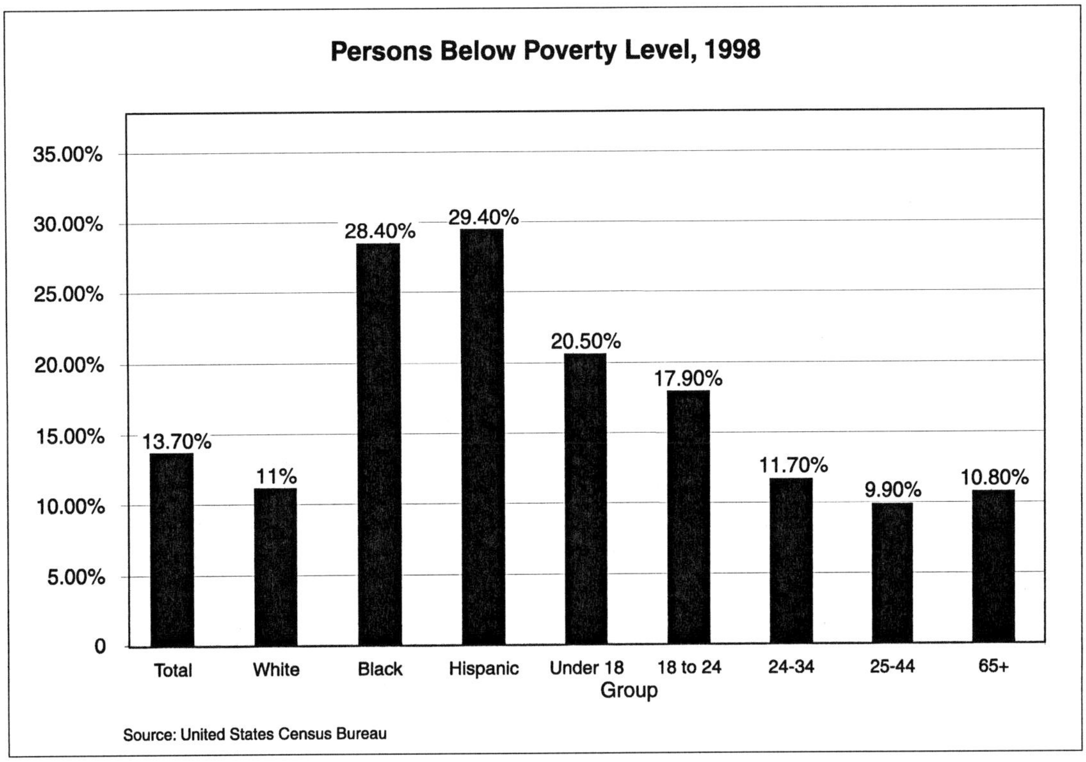

The Pressing Question

7. Considering the presence of poverty in the United States, is our welfare system a good idea? Elaborate on your view.

G. Distribution of Wealth

In measuring a person's economic status, the two yardsticks most often used are income and wealth. **Income** refers to the total amount of money earned during a given period. **Wealth** refers to the total amount of tangible assets that a person has accumulated at a given time. While someone may make $75,000 per year, they may have $250,000 in assets that include a car, half of a mortgage paid off, and various investments. A great amount of wealth can provide security that income alone cannot.

Does the existence of poverty mean that most Americans are poor? Questions like these are best approached by looking at the distribution of incomes in an economy. Take for instance country X. In this country, the lowest 20 percent of the population makes less than 5 percent of the income every year. On the other hand, the top fifth makes 42.7 percent of all the income. This kind of inequality was noticed by Karl Marx. He advocated a revolution of society that would strive to create a perfectly equal distribution of wealth and income.

With the growth of the world's population, and most people in the world living in underdeveloped countries, what will become of these new billions of people?

One device that economists use to demonstrate the distribution of wealth in a society is the **Lorenz Curve**. In his ideal society, Marx wanted all people to have the same amount of income and wealth. Notice that 40 percent of the population owns 40 percent of the wealth. But in most societies, the distribution of income is far from equal. Notice that the curve that is shown shows a society where 40 percent of the population get only about 10 percent of the income. In this society as well, 80 percent of the population gets only 40 percent of the income. This kind of income distribution creates vast relative poverty. Sometimes, it can cause civil strife and discontent.

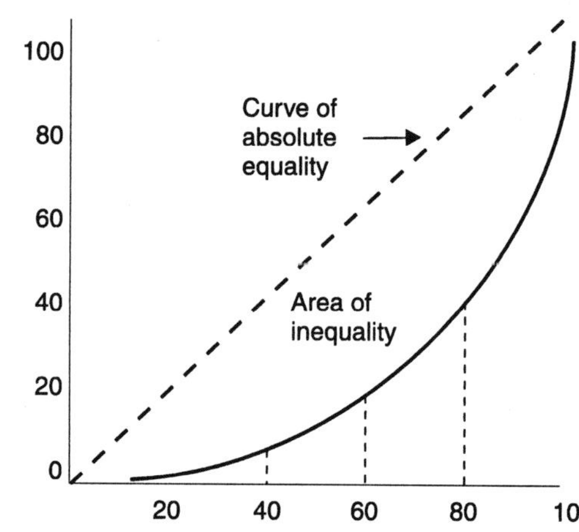

While the income distribution in the United States has become more equalized in the past century, the distribution of wealth remains greatly disparate between the upper and lower classes. In free-market economies, wealth can be distributed very unevenly. For instance, in the United States, the top 1 percent of the population owns about 20 percent of the private wealth. In less developed countries, that same 1 percent can own a much higher percentage. A country where 1 percent of the population owns upwards of 80 percent of the wealth may create social problems like poverty. People will resent their situation and perhaps rebel.

The question remains, "Can anything be done about this?" Our government tries to maintain somewhat of a balance through government programs and various transfer payments, but in a less developed country where the government is corrupt, the situation will continue. The leaders are often members of the rich elite and have a lot to lose if the status quo is not maintained. You need to decide what is moral and immoral. These answers are not absolute. This might lead into

This house is in an inner city neighborhood.

a good discussion of equity versus equality; is an unequal distribution of income and wealth equitable? Is an unequal distribution of income inequitable? If everyone has the same income and wealth, what are the incentives for people to be doctors, plumbers, garbage collectors? Who would decide what occupations certain people would have? Would we get the best doctors? Would we need lawyers (since everyone would get the same income and wealth)? Who would save? Why?

The Pressing Questions

8. Is the current distribution of wealth in the United States a problem? Why or why not?

9. If everyone in our society had the same amount of wealth and income, how might that adversely impact our economy?

H. The New Economy

We are living in a time of extraordinarily rapid change. New technology is changing the way we live and see the world around us. It seems as soon as we get used to one form of technology like VHS tapes, a new form like DVDs step in to take their place. One fact of our modern lives is that our economic behaviors change. We must adjust constantly.

In recent years, economists have been discussing something called "the new economy." Historically, the United States stumbled from recession to recession while citizens suffered periodic unemployment, rampant inflation, and poverty. In the 1990s, however, our country experienced almost an entire decade of economic growth. Not only was this unprecedented, but also economists could not explain it adequately.

There are some new facts that defy our knowledge of traditional modern economies. In the past, when productivity rose and the economy got hot, inflation usually followed. This was not the case in the 1990s. Also in the past, when there is structural change in the economy like we have at the turn of this new century moving from industry to service, there is usually a recession or massive unemployment. This is not the case either. Massive layoffs by major corporations in the United States have been offset by the creation of hundreds of thousands of new service-sector jobs. There is definitely something new to all of this. Is it possible for the economy to grow, not for five years at a time, but for ten or even twenty? Conventional knowledge argues against it, predicting a downturn at some point, but that reality has not materialized. Perhaps we have learned some economic lessons over the last two hundred years during which capitalism has existed.

Where do you fit into all of this? Your first job is to find what you like to do and to pursue a career in it. Another bad scenario involves you not being able to find a job or adequate educational opportunity. Or, after high school, you take a job for no other reason than it is offered to you. Getting a paycheck seems appealing to begin with, but five years down the road, you realize that you do not like what you do for a living. You would also see those who have more education than you pass you up on the career track. But because of your situation, you are stuck. You must think about where you want to be five to ten years from now. What will make you happiest? Remember, choose a job you enjoy, not just one that pays you well. Set sound goals, and work to achieve them.

You are part of a large, prosperous, and growing economy. In order to compete effectively, you need a good education and saleable skills. Familiarize yourself with technology and computers. They are the tools of our "new economy" and the major reason for our country's recent prosperity. Work hard and you will accomplish your goals.

The reality is that in most cases, if someone is willing to work hard, he or she has the opportunity to succeed in this country. You need to decide what success means to you. Good luck to you in making your way in our economy.

The Pressing Question

10. What are some of the hard realities for young people heading into the workplace today?

Name________________________

Date________________________

Reading and Vocabulary

Directions: Complete each of the following sentences with boldfaced words or information you found in your reading.

1. The United States, Canada, and Mexico freely trade between their borders because of a trade agreement called ____________________.

2. Paul got hired directly out of college at an ____________________ of $35,000 per year.

3. Her accumulated ____________________ included her assets of land, stock, bonds, and cash bank accounts.

4. The United States ____________________ more than it exports. Therefore, we have a trade ____________________ .

5. GATT was a trade agreement that eliminated some ____________________ , or taxes on imports, between the United States and many Asian countries.

6. Karl Marx believed that the workers, or what he called the ____________________ had throughout history been victims of abuse from the bourgeoisie.

7. Many people in developing nations like El Salvador live on what they grow in a system of ____________________ agriculture.

8. The United States currently has about ____________________ percent of the world's population, but we consume a considerable amount of the world's resources.

9. ____________________ poverty is worse than absolute poverty, because people can see the condition of their existence and may experience psychological hardship along with physical.

Name________________________

Date________________________

10. ____________________ is a system in which the factors of production are owned by people in the private sector.

11. Since the Cuban Revolution, the United States has enforced a strict ____________________ on the island nation and effectively stopped Cuban goods from making it to America shores.

12. Governments in countries like Sweden and France take a large role in the economy while allowing people to vote for their leaders in a system called ____________________ socialism.

13. Most business schools across the country teach courses on ____________________, in which students are expected to learn the damaging effects of immoral behavior in the marketplace.

14. Most Americans have heated houses, expendable income, and plenty of food due to our country's remarkable productivity and the ____________________ of living it creates.

15. A ____________________ economic system attempts to redistribute the wealth of a country evenly among all of the citizens.

16. The poverty line for a family of four in the United States is ____________________ or below.

Fundamentals of Economics
Lesson 37
Handout 43

Name________________________

Date________________________

Global Perspectives

Directions: Research a country from an assigned area of the world. Use the Internet, a current encyclopedia, or a recent world almanac to fill in the chart with the appropriate information. Make sure your information is current (i.e., within the last year or two).

Africa	Asia	Latin America
Middle East	Eastern Europe	Western Europe

Source ____

1. Country

2. Current Head of State

3. Famous Figures in History

4. Geography

5. Main Exports

6. #1 Industry

7. GDP

8. Per Capita GDP

9. Current Population

10. Type of Economic System

11. Currency Name

12. Currency in U.S. Dollars

13. From the information you gathered, how does a person from the country you researched differ in lifestyle from someone from the United States?

Name____________________________

Date____________________________

Economists' Views

Directions: Use an outside source such as an encyclopedia or other reference book, to fill in the following information about your assigned economist.

Adam Smith	Karl Marx	Ralph Nader	J. M. Keynes
Robert Malthus	J. B. Say	Thorstein Veblen	

Source: ____

1. Name
2. Years
3. Education

4. Famous Publications

5. Main Ideas and Theories

6. Brief Biography

7. Significance of the Ideas

8. Any Famous Friends of

Name____________________________

Date_____________________________

Ethical Dilemmas

Directions: Someone has done something ethically wrong in each of the following scenarios. For each situation, tell

- what was done wrong
- why it was wrong
- who the victim was

Be careful: One situation is perfectly ethical. See if you can guess which one.

1. Someone buys a stereo that was stolen from a local mall.

2. In a desperate situation, one student copies someone else's old term papers.

3. A group of teens has a huge and rowdy party at the house of a friend whose parents are out of town.

4. A bunch of people sneak into a theatre door that was unknowingly left open.

5. A company sells its product as a "giant quart." They are within the laws of the state. But research shows that people think that the bottle is bigger than a quart.

6. A change machine is giving five dollars in change for one dollar bills.

Name____________________________

Date____________________________

7. You have a library book that is way overdue, but they've stopped hassling you about it.

8. A lawyer defends someone that he or she knows is guilty.

9. A business fires a fifty-two year-old employee and replaces him with a younger, chcaper replacement.

10. A business executive falsifies numbers in an annual report to keep investors happy.

11. People on a bus fake injuries after a small accident in order to collect on insurance.

12. Someone leaks private information regarding a company before it is made public.

13. A construction inspector takes a bribe to keep quiet about some shoddy materials used in a new stadium.

Name________________________

Date________________________

My Beliefs

Directions: Write a few sentences that explain what you believe about each of the following topics. Try to sum up the principle by which you live and see the world in each category. Follow the example.

Chocolate Ice Cream Sundaes

I believe people should enjoy ice cream in moderation. People should not stop eating ice cream; they just should not eat it all the time.

Work

Possessions

Profit

Charity

Taxes

Government Programs

Prosperity

Federal Reserve

Politics

Racism

Ethics

Poverty

Retirement

Bibliography

Books

Arnold, Roger A. *Economics in Our Times*. Minneapolis: West Publishing Company, 1995.

Boris, Eileen, and Nelson Lichtenstein, eds. *Major Problems in the History of American Workers*. Lexington: D. C. Heath and Company, 1991.

Marx, Karl, and Friedrich Engels. *The Communist Manifesto*. Edited by Joseph Katz. New York: Washington Square Press, 1964.

O'Connor, David E. *Economics: Free Enterprise in Action*. Orlando: Harcourt Brace Jovanovich, 1984.

Starr, Isidore, et al. *Living American Documents*. New York: Harcourt Brace Jovanovich, 1971.

Welch, Patrick J., and Gerry F. Welch. *Economics: Theory and Practice*. Fort Worth: The Dryden Press, 1995.

Woll, Peter, ed. *American Government: Readings and Cases*. Boston: Little, Brown and Company, 1984.

Web Sites

PoliSci.com: The Political Reference Almanac
http://www.polisci.com/almanac/almanac.htm

Provides statistics and information about economic and political situations in the United States and around the world.

The Washington Post
http://www.washingtonpost.com

Updated daily with the latest social, political, and economic information.

The U.S. Census Bureau
http://www.census.gov

Supplies information about the latest economic indicators, income, poverty, foreign trade statistics, etc.

The Bureau of Economic Analysis
http://www.bea.doc.gov

Provides regional, national, and international data related to GDP; overview of U.S. economy including related data and articles.

The United Nations
http://www.un.org

Compiles information related to the United Nations, issues on the UN agenda, economic and social development, international law, humanitarian affairs, etc.

Bureau of Labor Statistics
http://www.bls.gov

Provides information on the economy—employment statistics and archive, industrial statistics and related data.

U.S. House of Representatives
http://www.house.gov

Contains access to bills and resolutions currently under consideration, events taking place on the House floor, and a directory of House office Web sites.

The White House
http://www.whitehouse.gov

Gives information about the current administration, links to pages about current issues in government and the economy.

Board of Governors of the Federal Reserve System
http://www.federalreserve.gov

Describes the Federal Reserve's duties; provides information on monetary policy, the banking system, regulation and supervision, and other areas related to the Fed.

Acknowledgments

For permission to reprint all works in this volume, grateful acknowledgment is made to the following holders of copyright, publishers, or representatives.

Lesson 7, Handout 7

For use of the United Way logo. Reprinted by permission of the United Way of America.

Lesson 7, Handout 8

For use of figures for Top Corporations According to Sales, 2000 and Top Public Corporations According to Profits, 2000. Reprinted by Permission of Forbes Magazine © 2000 Forbes.

Lesson 25, Handout 29

For use of two political cartoons. TOLES © 1998 The Buffalo News. Reprinted by Permission of UNIVERSAL PRESS SYNDICATE. All rights reserved.